Uncommon
Vol. III
A Glass Unbroken

Revised Version

Based on True Events

By Mel King

Plus, a Bonus Feature

"The Museum & Rose Garden"

Copyright © 2025 by Mel King

All rights reserved.

No part of this publication may be reproduced, distributed, or transmitted in any form or by any means, including photocopying, recording, or other electronic or mechanical methods, without the prior written permission of the publisher, except as permitted by copyright law.

Orlando - April 1985

Since I needed a car in Orlando, I drove across country with my father-in-law. We made an eight hour stop in Houston to see my college roommate Gil, who had moved to Houston a few years prior. It took us 64 hours and about $98 in gas to make the journey from LA to Orlando.

Martin Marietta
Finance Manager

I joined the Martin Marietta Corporation (MMC aka Martin) in April, 1985, and as usual, there were only a handful of Black managers, out of a total employment population of 15,000. I hired in at a Labor Grade 50, which is designated as a full Manager position; and, is rare to have someone hire in at this level. The next grade would be a director. The LG-50 is often coveted since it is the first management level that comes with a private office and an assigned parking spot.

My first assignment at Martin was the Pershing Missile program. This was a medium range atomic ballistic missile that was deployed in Germany and other European countries. It is strongly believed that the accuracy of this missile contributed to the demise of the Cold War and the tearing down of the Berlin Wall. Russian bunkers could withstand an atomic blast within a half mile of the bunker; the Pershing could deliver its payload within a few yards. The Pershing program was a large program and I was one of several Finance Managers reporting into a senior manager. Within the first two weeks being on the job, taking different sub-program production charts, I developed some cost projections for the program. This analysis and subsequent charts were similar to the Project  Control charts I developed while at Hughes Aircraft as an Industrial Engineer. I submitted the reports to the senior manager and pointed out some areas that were borderline in making profit, and others that were doing really well. The next day I was visited by a couple of Directors and got bombarded with questions as to how I got the information I presented, especially since I had just joined the company. What I presented gave them more and better information than what they were receiving, but they were more concerned about whether I had made

unauthorized access to financial data. Once they were satisfied about their concerns, they showed little interest in the reports. I was told later that it was a case of "Not invented here."

There were about 20 people in the group I was working with and, each month, we had two people spending a whole week preparing a report that went to Redstone Arsenal in Alabama. After witnessing the time spent preparing this report, I got with the team to see if I could help out. They were using Lotus 123, a program similar to Excel, to compile and report the data. (Just a note. I believe Lotus 1-2-3 was a superior program than Excel, Microsoft just had a better marketing strategy). I was extremely familiar with Lotus and proceeded to develop a program using "Macros" that would automate many of the manual functions. It took me almost a week to develop it. When I gave it to the team to try out, they were amazed. Many of the managers at MMC had very little experience with a PC, let alone having the capability to develop and use macros. A week later the team tried it out for real. They completed the report in two days, with much greater accuracy. It didn't take long before it became known to the rank and file that I was a no-nonsense Finance Manager, a straight shooter no less.

When I arrived in Orlando, I met two very special people, actually, one was a family whose last name also happened to be King. Although we never met previously, Jim and Dee use to live in LA and also went to Crenshaw Christian Center. They have three children, Andrita, Dexter, and Anissa. We bonded immediately and I was quickly adopted into the family and eventually, they into mine. One of the things that helped with the bonding was their Tuesday Night Bible Studies. I wanted to make sure I had some accountability, being so far and so long from home, that I made it a point to meet with them on Tuesdays and attend the studies. I began to attend church with them on Sundays as well.  The other person was Brian, he was a real estate agent. When I contacted the office in which he worked, and told them I was looking for an apartment, no one stepped up, except Brian. All the other agents didn't want to waste their time with a rental. However, Brian was very outgoing, and he saw this as another opportunity to meet someone. He met with me, showed me around and helped me get a very nice apartment. Brian's effort paid big dividends for him later.

After about nine months on the Pershing program, I was given a lead Finance Manager (FM) assignment, a sub-munitions dispensing missile that was a joint venture between France, Germany, Britain, and the U.S. In January 1986 I moved to my new office, it was on the east side of Orlando, in a 12-story high rise. I was on the ninth floor.

I said to one of the longtime occupants, "Wow, I think this building will provide an excellent view of any launch from Cape Canaveral, it's only 45 miles away."

"Yeah Mel, you can see it about five seconds after liftoff. It's a great view."

In Florida, because it is so flat, once you get above the tree line, a person can see for miles. For the nine months I had been in Orlando, I never saw a space shuttle launch. It just so happened that the first month of my being in my new office, the space shuttle Challenger was scheduled to be launched. I was going to be in an excellent location to see the launch.

At the time of the launch, many of us gathered in the common area and looked out of the window that faced eastward. We had the radio on to listen to the countdown " ..3..2..1. We have ignition. We have liftoff." It was only about three seconds after the words, we have liftoff, that we were able to see the shuttle. It was a clear cold day, and because of that, the shuttle seemed magnified. We watched the

Lot Space Shuttle Challenger
January 1986 **1986**

shuttle rise on a plume of smoke, that almost looked like a string of pearls smashed together.

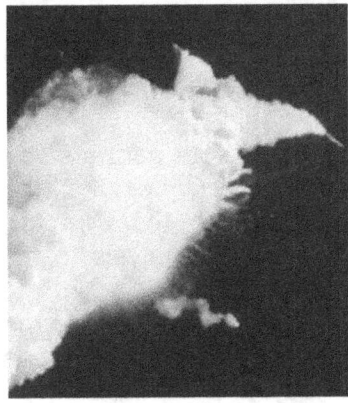

"Wow, what a sight. Look at that."
"What a thrill ride that must be."
"Amazing that we can do something like that."

As we watched, I saw the rocket boosters separate. I said out loud, "The boosters aren't supposed to separate until about two minutes into the flight. That separation seemed a little too soon."

Although I had not seen a shuttle launch, I did know a little about its flight characteristics.

"You know Mel, I think you're right. It is too soon for booster separation. I hope nothing is wrong."

At that very moment, we heard the announcer on the radio say that the Challenger had experienced a malfunction. Many of us who were alive that day will always remember that fateful moment.

I wasn't on the program too long before the Program Director (PD) and I began to have issues with one another. I began to see areas where I believed potential overruns existed and wanted to identify this in my monthly report to Finance. The Program Director didn't want the info reported, at least not yet. His comment was that there is a "potential" overrun and that it hasn't happened yet. It was during this time that I received a very fateful call from one of the VPs. The VP knew I had worked at Hughes Aircraft and wanted to know if I knew a guy named Earl that works for Hughes. I told him that I did, and that Earl was one of the Program Managers I worked for on the Roland project. I gave him my opinion and said I thought the company would do well to pick him up. What I wasn't aware of was that MMC had been very close to being banned from doing business with the Government due to poor quality control. Martin Marietta needed fresh blood to come in, clean house and begin to right the many wrongs. I told him I thought Earl could do it. Earl was ultimately hired. When Earl arrived, I contacted him and put him in touch with Brian, the real estate agent. By the way, Brian got the deal on our home; Earl's home, and, subsequent referrals from Earl as he brought in fresh blood to overhaul the Quality organization.

As the months went by, I began to observe some things that began to make me really have cost concerns about the program; and not just "potential." I brought my concerns to the Program Director.

"Jason, I am really concerned about the numbers. My analysis indicates that we are already in a projected overrun position and if we don't do something now, it will get much worse," I said.

"Mel, we are starting to get better cooperation with our partners so I believe our expenditures will begin to decrease; and besides, the projections you show, we can't be that bad." Jason, the Director, however, didn't believe my numbers. I then took my analysis to my direct line of management, the Finance Director and showed him my concerns. The Finance Director called a meeting with the PD and me to discuss the numbers. As we were sitting in the Finance Director's office, the PD denied that I had either mentioned the potential overrun or that I had shown him the numbers.

"Mel, I don't recall you ever showing me numbers that would indicate that we are in an over-run or possible over-run condition." The Program Director said.

I didn't argue, I politely asked for the documents the Finance Director was holding.

"May I have the cost documents please?
The Finance Director gave me the papers.

I flipped through the pages and then looked at the PD, "Is this not your signature?" I asked.

Jason could not deny that it was his signature Now, whether he read it or not, that was up to him. My duty was to make sure he got the report. To this day, this is very puzzling to me. My job was to manage the finances of the program. I saw a potential financial problem and brought it to the attention of the Program Director and then the Finance Director. Somehow, I got the feeling that I was being made out to be the bad guy. The Program Director got upset because I went to the Finance Director. It didn't matter that I brought it to his attention first... and he chose to ignore the warning. Now, with Finance, I would get in trouble if I detected a problem and did not report it. So, how is it that I detect an issue, earlier than most Finance Managers would do so, and I get in trouble for reporting it? What I suspect is that the Program Director was aware but thought he could fix the problem on his time scale. What I did was to surface the issue, it got attention, and now it was no longer the Program Director's timetable. (Could it be that his bonus may be impacted?) When I was assigned to the program, I now wonder if they thought I would be smart enough to catch the potential issue. After all, several FMs before me had not discovered what I saw; and, I saw the problem within a few days of my arrival on the program. As it turned out, because of my early warning, we were able to avert a financial catastrophe on the program. However, from that moment on, the PD never felt comfortable in my presence. I knew my time on the program was going to be short.

A New Opportunity

"God works in mysterious ways."

After my meeting with the Program and Finance Director, the relationship with the PD and I was somewhat strained. It wasn't too long afterwards that I get a call from Earl, saying he would like to have lunch with me. I'm thinking he wants to rekindle the friendship from L.A. and to ask about my thoughts of Martin Marietta. While at lunch, Earl begins to talk about what he has seen, in his early exposure to Martin Marietta, as the Quality Director.

"You know Mel you could have told me it was going to be this challenging. Did you know that Martin was about to lose its ability to contract with the Government? There were so many findings the Government stopped their last audit midway through and went home. The Quality and manufacturing elements I know I can handle. What I am most concerned about are the overruns. Every program we have looks to be in an overrun condition, many of them seem to be fairly significant."

I'm listening the whole time with an occasional, "I see," or "What do they expect you to do about that?" when Earl poses the question,

"How would you like to come work for me; and, what would you do to help work the financial problem?"

I sat back in my chair, became very meditative, and then said:

"There are about four things I would do up front. One, if you want something to improve, measure it. Two, establish accountability." And then I paused.

Earl noticing my pause said, "What of the other two?"

"Those two and others come with the package."

Earl began to laugh.

He said, "That is why I wanted to talk with you. You're a thinker. If it's OK with you, I'll talk to your bosses and see if I can get you to come work with me."

"Right now, I don't think that's going to be too much of a problem."

"Why is that?"

I told Earl what happened about exposing the potential over-run; and, instead of being rewarded, I was being made out to be the bad guy.

"What you just told me only makes me believe you are the *right* guy. I need someone who is going to be honest and straight forward. That's the only way I can see us getting out of this. How soon do you think you can get off the program?"

"Once you get the go-ahead, I would say, give me three days to bring the new guy up to speed. After that, I can be on call if they need me."

"Good. I can use you right away. I'm going to talk to your boss as soon as I get back. We are going to start budget negotiations with Finance in a couple of weeks and I want you to lead the charge."

Silver Willow Court
A House that was our Home

As Renee and I toured Orlando for housing, we saw a limited number of two-story homes. Those we did see had the master bedroom

My mom and Aaron on the empty

on the ground floor. We wanted all the bedrooms upstairs, except for the guest bedroom. We worked with a contractor to design our home and the swimming pool. The house was 3400 square feet, five bedrooms with three and a half baths, swimming pool and a Jacuzzi, situated on two thirds of an acre. It was a great home. The half bath was between two of the bedrooms. This half bath ultimately became "Dez's bathroom" and Aaron and Darien were relegated to the hall bath. Ladies can be possessive about bathrooms. I suspect that if we, Renee and I didn't have a double sink, I would be joining Aaron in the hall bath. Renee and I had a screened-in balcony outside our bedroom, that overlooked the pool, with French double doors. My study was a small room with a half wall that overlooked the family room. In the family room was a two-story brick fireplace. One of the things that the kids thought was really cool was the laundry chute. Renee's closet was right above the laundry room, so we had the contractor put in a chute that permitted us to dump laundry right in the basket downstairs. It was great. The house was located on the southwest side of Orlando, about three miles from Universal Studios and about 12 miles from Disney World.

First Weekend at Silver Willow Court

We settled the mortgage contract and moved into our home during the week. It was our first weekend in our new home, and the first time I had a chance to sleep in, since I am up and gone by 6:30 AM during the week. It was a fall day, we had the screened-in balcony, double French

doors open, a cool breeze was coming in, and the sun was bright and shiny. I was in that twilight stage of early morning sleep when I began to hear a strange noise. Mind you, it was a brand-new house, first time I'm sleeping this late, and I have no idea what the noise is or where it's coming from. Also, being the man of the house, I'm the one getting up, while Renee is lying in bed, willing to let me sacrifice my body for the cause. As the fog from my brain began to clear, it soon registered that the sound was not consistent, making it a little more difficult to locate. Initially, I went to the bedroom door, and since I was in my birthday suit, I just poked my head out. I didn't want to run into the kids.

As I was listening for some kind of sound down the hallway, the noise seemed to be getting louder and therefore, more easily to locate. It was coming from behind me. Strange. At this time, it is important that you know where our house was located. We were the seventh home to be built in this 100+ acre development. The only house near us was our neighbor, whom we could not see out any back window or door. A half mile away was an orchard, and a half mile beyond that was the turnpike, which was below ground level. Our bedroom was on the  second floor, the balcony overlooked the pool and faced rearward. So, with confidence of privacy I headed to the balcony in my birthday suit. Just as I got to the doors, a hot air balloon with 4-5 people in it was traversing through our back yard, descending in preparation to land. They were of equal height to our balcony and our bedroom. Me, I'm framed by the French doors, not expecting to see anyone, let alone seeing someone, eyeball to eyeball. They saw me, and with a huge grin, just began waving.

I think one of them said, "It is a fine morning, isn't it?"

I'm not sure what was said since I did a quick 'bout face. We had an oversized bedroom and it seemed like it was taking forever to get to the safety of the bed and its welcoming covers. Renee had woken up just a few moments earlier, was under cover and wide awake to observe my encounter and my embarrassment with the hot air balloon and its occupants. We found out later that Saturday was a big day for

ballooners; and, our subdivision, with its paved streets and wide-open lots, were a cherished landing spot. We didn't know, since it was our first Saturday in the house. That same afternoon, we took the kids to get a bite to eat. We were sitting by the window and wouldn't you know it, a couple of trucks pull in with a hot air balloon in tow (deflated of course). As the kids were eating, Renee had this silly grin on her face and still chuckling. I didn't have to ask what she was smiling and chuckling about.

"Wonder if they've been to our neighborhood, today?" Renee said to no one in particular. Even today, many years later, the sound of a hot air balloon, when the gas is ignited with its resultant sound and flame, automatically brings back a wanting to forget memory.

The Neighborhood

We were never short of out-of-town guests while living in Orlando. We had gone to Disney and Universal Studios so often that when friends came, we gave them the keys to the extra vehicle, pointed them in the direction they should go and said, "Have fun." With the pool Jacuzzi, bedroom with adjoining bath, many of our friends said our home was better than a hotel, hence it became known as "The King's Inn." We had great neighbors, all of which we stay in contact with today. There are about 100 homes in the Willow Woods development, and as par for the course, we were the only Black family in residence. After about four years, another Black family moved in.

There would be times, early on Saturday mornings when I would be cleaning the pool and one of our neighbor's daughter, Shannon, would come over. She would open the screen door to the pool area and walk in.

"Hello Mr. Thing" she says.
"Hi Shannon."
"Is Desiree up?"
"No, she is still sleeping."
"Ok."

Then she would proceed into the kitchen area where she would get a bowl, cereal, milk and sit down at the table. She would sit there until Desiree came down from upstairs. She was no more than four years old. Shortly the phone would ring, her mom is on the phone.

"Hi Mel, Is Shannon over there?"
"Yep"
"OK, thanks."

Her mom, Jeannie, was satisfied that Shannon was somewhere "safe" and wasn't concerned about her.

Shannon would be with Desiree most of the morning.

This was such a wholesome neighborhood I don't have enough space to tell you all the great things that happened while living in this home. It was nothing for neighbors to borrow a cup of sugar, couple of eggs, or mow the lawn of a neighbor if they were out of town for the weekend. At Christmas, the kids went caroling from house to house. There were times when I came home from work, when Bob, our other neighbor would be playing catch with his daughter. I would get my mitt and join them. It wouldn't be long before there was 8 - 9 of us hitting pop ups. The same thing may happen if we had the barbeque grill going. There would be a spontaneous barbeque party as neighbors would bring something to add to the growing gathering. This was a neighborhood where not only the kids knew one another, the parents did as well.

The Word – Being a Witness

Upon arrival in Orlando, I quickly sought out a Bible Study group in which I could fellowship mid-week. As it turned out, I met up with a minister, Jim, who used to attend Crenshaw Christian Center in Los Angeles, and his last name also happened to be King (no relations). His family members (his wife, Delores, his daughters, Andrita and Anissa, and son, Dexter) quickly became my family away from home. I didn't know him in L.A. but my sister did, and, it was through Vic, that Jim and I got together. After about four months of attending their Tuesday night Bible Study, I suggested that they start a church. It took two more months of discussions before they were convinced enough to begin the planning to hold Sunday Worship services. Couple of weeks prior to the first Sunday meeting, Jim, myself and several others were going out into nearby neighborhoods, handing out flyers, promoting the new ministry, Orlando Faith Christian Center.

The next Saturday, Jim and I paired up to canvas a neighborhood. We were going two by two, but the day was getting away from us so we decided to pass out the remaining few flyers as individuals. Jim and I parted. After about 15 minutes, I saw Jim coming my way.

"Hey Mel, I need you to come with me."

"OK. What's up? I said."

"I met this couple, or at least the woman wants to talk more about the church and our ministry. I thought it best that I come back to get you since we may be invited into the house."

"That's great Jim. How far away is it?

"Not far, only a couple of blocks."

So off we went. I'm all excited about getting an opportunity to present the Word. Now this is why we were out in the streets. Hallelujah.

"Oh, Mel, I guess I should tell you, her husband or her boyfriend, I don't know which he is, well, he has a shotgun right next to the door."

At about that time I did a little stutter step.

"A what?"

"A shotgun."

OK, I can recognize a test when I see one. Am I committed to serving the Lord, only when times are good, or, am I willing to put myself in harm's way if need be? I didn't say much to Jim on the way, I just began praying in the Spirit. Jim didn't say much either. I suspect he was praying as well. This attitude of prayer continued all the way to the couple's house. Jim approached the door. It was do or die time (and the dying could be taken literally). Jim knocked on the door.

"Oh, you're back." The man said.

"Do you mind if we come in?" Jim said.

"No, I guess not."

Well, we made it past phase I, getting in the door without getting our heads blown off. As we entered the house, the man turned around to go sit on a sofa. And true enough, he had a shotgun next to the door. I casually, but purposely stood between him and the shotgun. Jim addressed the lady.

"We will keep this short. Have you ever accepted Jesus as your personal Lord and Savior?" Jim asked.

"No, I have not." She responded.

"OK, let me tell you a few things about Jesus, who he is, what he did for you, and what benefits we have in him. After that I would like to say, what is called, 'The Sinner's Prayer' with you."

Jim gave a brief outline of the Gospels and came to a conclusion with the question,

"Would you like to say the sinner's prayer?"

"Yes, I would."

"OK. Repeat after me."

Jim began the Sinner's Prayer, and the lady repeated every line, word for word; except, when it came time to repeat the name of Jesus and declaring him as her Savior.

"Come on repeat after me. I declare Jesus Christ as my Lord and Savior. . . "

"I declare . . . . " She would say and stop.

I continued to pray in the Spirit.

"Come on you can do it. I declare Jesus Christ as my Lord and Savior. . . ." Jim would say again.

"I declare . . . "

Jim, being a little frustrated just instinctively reached out and laid hands on her forehead. She collapsed on the floor. Her boyfriend jumped up off the sofa.

"What did you do to her? What did you do to her?" He cried excitedly.

Once again, I made sure I was in-between him and the shotgun as I responded.

"Pastor Jim laid hands on your wife; and, ...:

"She's not my wife, we are not married yet."

"OK. Anyhow, Pastor Jim laid hands on her and what you saw happening to her was Holy Spirit coming upon her."

"Now I don't want no demons or evil spirits or any of that crap coming upon her."

"No. What you see is her being comforted by the Holy Ghost. Look at the smile on her face. You wouldn't see a smile like that if she was encountering demons, now, would you?

"No, I guess not," he said.

After about two minutes laying out on the floor, we help her rise to her feet.

"Now repeat after me. I declare Jesus Christ as my Lord and Savior. . . "Jim says.

"I declare Jesus Christ as my Lord and Savior. . . " She says.

The transformation was amazing. Prior to her having hands laid upon her she couldn't even mention the name of Jesus. Now, she is unabashedly declaring Him as Lord and Savior. This transformation was not lost upon her male companion.

"What you guys did for her; do you think you can do for me? You wouldn't believe it, but I used to be a minister myself. I used to be a Baptist preacher. I kinda backslid, but I still love the Lord."

"The Lord is no respecter of persons, what He did to and for her, he can do to and for you." Jim said.

We spent another half hour with them, talking about the scriptures, led him to the Lord, and encouraged them to come to church Sunday. They came that Sunday; however, they didn't continue in their efforts as they were not seen again after the third visit.

Interacting with the Kids – Big & Small

As the kids got older, Aaron became of age where he needed to learn how to ride a bike. I brought him and his new bike outside for the "boy to man" ritual of learning how to ride. Aaron was extremely resistant and said that he didn't want to learn how to ride a bike. Renee was watching out the dining room window as she saw her son begin to cry. She took it for about 10 minutes, then she came running outside.

"What are you doing to my boy?"

"I am doing nothing that is going to hurt him," I said.

I put my arms around her shoulder, turned her back toward the house, and patted her on the rear.

"Go, do something to be busy and stop watching. We will be here all day until he learns."

He learned how to ride that day.

Desiree was an athlete at a very early age. At one time a golf and tennis pro both wanted to work with her. We were not in favor of her losing a lot of her childhood for the training that we knew would be necessary; however, we let her decide. She chose to be a kid. Good for her. She did become the high scorer in a church league for the girls' soccer team. I coached the team for about three years.

During the summer months we would have water fights around the house. It would start out with about six of us, our family and my nephew's family. Once the fight started, the neighbor's kids, Eddie, Shannon, Lindsey, and Stephanie would come join the fight. From there it wouldn't take long before the adults got into the fray. Many times, the line would quickly blur as to who was on who's side. It often became  a free for all. These water fights got to be so well known that some of our friends, that didn't live in the neighborhood, would call to find out when was the next Water Fight Saturday.

I recall on one instance, Phil, a very good friend of ours, whom Aaron and Dez call "Uncle Phil," (Phil was the host on Nick Arcade) and I had Dez in our crosshairs. She was outside of the "Safe zone" and had to pass by us to get to it. Phil and I both had four water balloons each in our hands or within easy grasp. The closest point Dez would come to us was about 15 feet. The house was a backdrop. Perfect kill zone. What happened next was like a movie put in *slow-motion*. Dez looked at Phil then at me, then she looked at the gate that offered a safe haven. It was easy to see the mental calculation she  was doing. Distance, speed, accuracy of thrown objects, (Phil and I were known for our lethality), etc. Dez took off running, hair streaming behind her, long legs grabbing for turf, and arms pumping. As Dez approached the kill zone, Phil and I let loose with a broad salvo. Keeping the movie camera allegory; the camera has a face-on shot of Phil and I, arm and hands just releasing the balloons, the balloons coming right at the camera and growing bigger as they approached the target. In your mind you can picture the inevitable... Desiree soaking wet with multiple impacts of water balloons. [Regular speed]. The camera shows all of the balloons hitting the side of the house. We reloaded and fired again...and missed again. Unbelievable! We missed with all eight balloons. You could see water marks all along the side of the house, wasn't a dry spot, but none touched Dez. To this day, Phil and I talk about that run that Dez made.

On another occasion, I am out washing my car when Dez and Eddie come out of the house through the garage trying to sneak up on me. They had a fairly small water rifle and intended to catch me unawares. Eddie was carrying the rifle. What they didn't know was that I had anticipated their attack and parked the car near the front of the house where I had pre-staged two big water cannons. As they approached, I feigned surrender.

"Now you guys wouldn't shoot an innocent person in cold blood, would you? Dez, for sure you wouldn't shoot your own dad?"

"Humm, let me think about it." She said, with a mischievous smile.

All the while I was talking, I had my hands raised, began backing up to the front of the car, which was near the front of the house. Once I got to the front of the house, I bent over, got the two, pre-charged water cannons.

"Ah, hah" I said.

And then I stood Rambo style, butt of the cannons on hip and barrels pointed up in the air. Eddie's reaction was priceless. Panic got ahold of him, so much so that he threw the water rifle down, turned and started running. Dez, since Eddie had the weapon, turned and ran alongside him, stride for stride, and hitting him on the shoulder, all the while yelling.

"What did you do that for? Why did you throw the rifle down? Huh. Why? Now what are we gonna do?"

I was laughing so hard I couldn't shoot if I wanted to. Eddie's reaction, unfortunately, is what happens sometimes in war. A soldier will get so scared, throw his weapon down and start running. Forgetting that the weapon is what can help save him.

Phil Moore is the "Big" in Big & Small Kids.

This guy would stop by the house, grab Aaron and Dez, along with his son and head off to the park or mall. They would be gone for hours. He was very uncouth, in that it didn't matter where we were or what we were doing, he would not let any situation get serious.

One evening while at a restaurant, with Phil and his wife Kathy, I said something to Aaron.

"Aaron, stop waving your spoon around, you're going to get food all in your hair, and maybe everybody else's," I said.

"Aaron, stop waving your spoon around, you're going to get food all in your hair, and maybe everybody else's." Phil said in a fairly close imitation of my voice. Of course, Aaron and Dez starts laughing. Then Dez, picks up her spoon and starts waving it around.

"Dez, don't you start it," I said.

"Dez, don't you start it," Phil says.

It went downhill from there as Renee picks up her spoon and starts waving it around.

"Renee, don't you start waving your spoon around, you're as bad as Aaron and Dez," I said.

"Renee, don't start waving your spoon around, you're as bad as Aaron and Dez," Phil says.

"Oh well, if you can't beat 'em, may as well join 'em."

I picked up my spoon and began waving it around. I'm sure the whole restaurant thought we were crazy. It was like that with Phil. One time, at the French Pavilion in Disney World, a group of us were having dinner when out of the blue, Phil starts acting like he knows French. He doesn't know French; however, a

French woman leaves a nearby table, comes over and with a very excited voice proclaims, "Finally, I am so glad someone can speak French." Then she begins to talk to Phil in French.

Of course, Phil had no clue what she was saying, and had to ultimately let the lady know. We would have laughed really hard had it not been for the utter dejection on the lady's face. The lady coyishly turns around and heads back to her table.

"See Phil, I told you your antics are gonna get you in trouble one day. It was funny though. We all had to try really hard not to laugh," I said.

A Gathering Place

Our home was a "gathering place," or, as my niece Marcia coined, "A Fun-Haven." A month didn't go by that we didn't have something going on. You would think that our neighbors would complain with so many things happening all the time. They didn't because they had a standing invitation to join us at any event. Many times, they did.

It was not an unusual occurrence that an impromptu "Hallelujah" session would start and last until 12 – 1:00 AM in the morning. Somebody would get on our piano, somebody else would go to their car, comeback with a guitar, and I don't know how so many tambourines mysteriously appeared.

: L – R, (adults) Victoria, sis; Keith, nephew; Elsie, mom; Amay, Renee's mom; Renee. Children: Darien, son; Desiree, behind Darien; Bree, Victoria's daughter; Ebony, Keith's daughter; Aaron.

"I had it just in case." They would say.

Odds were in their favor that something was going to happen. We always had a rowdy, rocking, worshiping good time.

One Labor Day weekend, Renee, Aaron and Dez were in L.A. when I had a friend call me. He was in Miami, just got off of a cruise with Crenshaw Christian Center, and wanted to come and spend the weekend with us. He told me that he and six other ladies were coming to Orlando, but the girls had reservations at a motel already, he did not. I offered for him to stay at the house. The girls were driving up, and he was catching a train. I picked him up on Thursday, late afternoon and that night, about 10:00 PM, he gets a phone call from his fiancé, one of the six ladies. The motel they booked was infested with roaches. They didn't want to stay there and wanted to know if I knew of any hotels they could go to. We called around, but at such late notice, in Orlando, on an upcoming Labor Day weekend, nada, nothing.

Since Renee and the kids were gone, except Darien, I offered them the opportunity to stay at our home that night and maybe something could be worked out the next day. They showed up at the house at about 11:30 PM. Things don't get sorted out until about 1:00 AM. I go to work at 6:30 AM. A short night. That Friday when I come home, my friend Richard approached me, at the request of the ladies.

"Do you think the girls can just stay here and not worry about a hotel?" He asked.

Humm, I wonder why? I had put them two to a room with essentially their own private bath. They had access to a pool, Jacuzzi, plenty of privacy, and no cockroaches.

I said, "Oh yeah, right, six ladies in the house while Renee is gone. Well, that will teach her to leave me alone."

We both laughed. True to form, I had some friends over for Barbeque that weekend so Richard and the six ladies had an opportunity to meet some other people while they were here. After the weekend, they all flew back to L.A., leaving with a good experience of Orlando.

As was said earlier, when living in Orlando, a person can always count on family and friends visiting throughout the year. There was hardly a month that would pass where we didn't have company. I don't know if you would consider sis, mom, mom in-law, nephew, company, but we sure saw them on a frequent basis while in Orlando.

I had my dependable yellow 626 Mazda of which most everyone had a nickname for, such as yellow mustard, yellow cab, and even baby poop made the list. The car however got me across country and provides daily transportation without problems; so, I don't care what they call it, just as long as they don't say it near my car. Anyhow, when friends or relatives come, Renee acts as chauffeur and drives everyone around in our Dodge Colt Vista, a seven-passenger micro van. Aaron

and Dez always welcomes company as it gives them an opportunity to go to Disney World, Busch Gardens, Sea World, and later, Universal Studio's multiple times over.

Quality Assurance
Developing a Viable Quality Business Organization

Earl was true to his word and spoke to my Finance Director upon his return from our lunch meeting. As I suspected, my boss was thrilled to have an opportunity to get in good graces with the Missile Program Director, of which I reported, by announcing that I will be moving to another program. The transfer happened very quickly. Earl moved me to an office adjacent to his on the sixth floor of the tower. The tower was seven stories, the Company President and his direct VP reports were on the seventh.

Because of the upcoming budget reviews with Finance and the work needed to be done for its preparation, my meeting with my direct reports was put off for a couple of weeks. I got together with the Quality Directors and Managers to review their budgets. I revamped the budgets, re-worded them, and re-packaged them. Together, myself and the Quality Directors, we went in to the budget reviews. I was the spokesperson. I think we did rather well. I know we did better than the Quality Directors thought; as I later found out, better than what Finance had planned. It was one of those "chance" meetings I came upon where two financial managers were talking about the recent budget reviews. They were unaware that I was nearby.

Later that day I saw Earl and relayed to him what I overheard.

"Hi Earl, do you have a minute or so? Just want to tell you something I overheard from a couple of Finance Managers.". I asked.

"Sure Mel, what's up?" Earl said.

I proceeded to tell him what I heard.

"You know, Quality did really good at that last budget review." One Manager said.

"Yeah, who would have thought?" The other Manager said.

"I think what was surprising to all of us was how quickly Mel came up to speed."

"Yeah, he wasn't there a week, and he comes in leading the discussions on every one of the groups. You know, I don't know why we didn't keep him in Finance."

"Well, he did a darn good job. We gave them more money than we thought we were going to. We even dipped into our reserves a little, and you know how much that hurt," they said.

"You know Earl, I was pleased to know that we made Finance feel a little pain; at least more than they expected," I said.

"Thank you, Mel. My guys told me how much they appreciated your help. But it doesn't stop there. We still have a lot more work to do."

My Team

Upon my first sessions with my supervisors and immediate reports, I laid down the ground rules in which we would operate as a unit, as a team.

"We are the gate keepers of the private lives of many of your associates. I will not and cannot tolerate violation of privacy, gossip, disclosure, or incomplete reporting of issues. I want the truth, the whole truth, and nothing but the truth," I said.

I would say that the majority of the team were skeptics. For the past 3 - 4 years, this whole group had been passed over for raises or promotions. I'm sure they were thinking;

"What is going to be different, other than perhaps more work and less fun."

I laid down our operational ground-rules and emphasized integrity, honesty, and ownership.

Understandably, there were 100% skeptics in the room of 26 people. I understood that I had to be aware of the hesitancy of some people to accept the leadership of a Black person; and the fact that those people may question ability, understanding, or experience of that Black person. I imagine some must have thought, how was I going to make a change when their former boss, who was part of the "Good ol' Boys" community, didn't do much for them.

The organizational structure had a Quality Manager (QM) for each program or several programs to each Quality Manager, depending on the size of the program. The QM had a staff of technical individuals and from one to three of my staff members handling the financial part of the program. In the past, not a lot of attention was given to the financial side. I wanted to change that, and I figured that I was going to make changes from the top. I got Earl to agree to hold monthly review meetings; one of the things that I withheld from telling him at our lunch meeting/ interview. Each Quality Manager was going to be held financially, as well as technically, accountable for their programs. This had not been done previously. I asked Earl to give us a month to prepare for the first meeting. With equal emphasis on finances, as well as technical, and since my staff was responsible for finances, it now elevated the importance of each of my staff members. The change in my staff was immediate and dramatic. At my staff's planning and prep session for the monthly meetings, the energy level was very high. The financial data gathering was my staff's responsibility and all of them accepted, no I would say, relished the opportunity to participate in a significant way. During the discovery and prep phase, it was determined that the total combined over-run on all Quality programs was around $14 million dollars. We were stunned. Of course, I had the job of presenting this to Earl. He in turn had the job of presenting it to the Company President. But I didn't let him present the numbers without an action plan, part of which, were the monthly review meetings, and a statement letting the QM's know that they will be held accountable.

Quality Reviews

Quality Review meetings were held in Earl's office. Earl had about six other individuals reporting to him that were Directors, plus myself as his Business Manager, in the room as each QM presented their report. The QM's had to present their budget, technical risks, and schedule. They in turn had to state how they are tracking to their budget, technical challenges and schedule. If they were deviating from either of the three, they had to have a plan developed to show how they were going to get back on track. Later, I would introduce Green-Yellow-Red indicators to identify the condition of the entity of which they were reporting. Green if nominal, Yellow if there was about a 5 -15% deviation, and Red for anything above 15%. At the end of each review, in the presence of Earl and his direct reports, every QM gave thanks for the help and support given them, by my staff, in preparation of the review. It was the beginning of a new era in the Quality organization. Even though there was a huge mountain to climb ($14M) there was a noticeable "can do" attitude exhibited by everyone. After the last QM presented his review and left, Earl looked at his staff.

"What do you think?" Earl said.

After some discussion, one Director summed it up;

"Although the numbers looked bleak, we all felt that it was a good review process, it was good to know what the numbers are exactly, and that we are putting things in place to reduce the numbers."

Surprisingly, not one Director made a comment to me or even implied credit to me for my having initiated the review process. I thought, "Sometimes it would be nice, even if once in a while, senior management or my peers would recognize the accomplishment of a significant event that was orchestrated by me." Why these reviews had not been done in the past, I don't know. The fact is they were not. Another fact is, as a result of these reviews, we started working down the projected over-run, from a $14 million projected over-run to an actual $200 thousand under-run in one year. A side benefit for my staff, and to the company, was that my staff got to be more closely aligned with their respective QMs.

It was about two months after the first Program Review that I had one of the QMs ask if it was possible to get a raise for one of my staff members. I didn't hesitate to put the paperwork in. Following the approval of the raise, I spoke to the Quality Manager.

"Would you mind being on stand-by and let me page you to come to the meeting. I would like to surprise Robert and I would like for you to present the paperwork, notifying him of his raise."

"Wow. No one has ever asked me to do that outside of my own staff. I would consider it an honor."

"OK. I'll page you to let you know when to come."

"No Problem."

During the meeting I surreptitiously paged the QM. I delayed a little bit, then asked Robert to come to the front of the room. The timing was perfect. Just as Robert came up front, the back door opened. The room got quiet when the QM 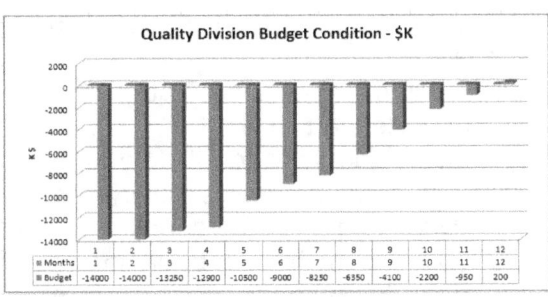 walked into the room. After all, my team had been beaten up so much and for so long that it was a "Now what!" situation. The QM played his part. He entered, stern faced, looking forward, directly at Robert. He raised the folder in his hand opened it, still stern faced.

"You are very much deserving of this and I am glad to be the one to give it to you." The QM said, still stern faced.

He then hesitated. It was quiet before, now, I don't think anyone was breathing. Then with a smile;

"It is a raise, effective next pay period. Thank you for a job well done."

The silence continued for a moment longer until it began to register what the QM said, then cheers, laughter, and clapping of hands erupted. It was the beginning thaw of the deep freeze for my staff. They had been ignored and rejected for so long, and now there was hope, a new beginning. I had the team for about four years and all but two of the team members, out of 26, either got out of cycle raises or a promotion. The two that didn't, from my assessment, had not displayed the energy, teamwork, or enthusiasm as their peers; and that was unfortunate.

Under the Bus

When it came time for yearly reviews for raises, we were about six months into the program review process. We were now showing about a $5 million-dollar reduction in the over-run. Earl asked for the chart that depicted the reduction. When he returned from the President's office, he was smiling pretty good. I had shown the same information to my Financial Management team (Martin had a matrix management system. Even though I reported to Earl on a daily basis, functionally, I reported to Finance) and there was very little in the way of recognition or acknowledgement. Had I been part of the "Good 'ol Boy" network, I am sure it would have been different. Maybe a promotion or at least a $10,000 bonus. That would have been a fair trade for saving the company $5 million. But in fact, at some point during this reduction campaign, my Financial Management team attempted to throw me under the bus. It started this way. One Thursday, Earl came into my office.

"Mel the President wants to meet with me and discuss the Quality financials. When do you think I can meet with him and go over the numbers?

"I will check and get back with you later today. But as soon as I find out, I'll let you know."

"Well, I am here to talk to you about it. So, how long do you think it will take to do the analysis and prepare the numbers?"

"Hu-u-u-mm, let me check a couple of things."

I pick up my budget book, look at a few things, then look at Earl.

"Earl, I can have something for you by Wednesday of next week."

"That long, huh?"

"I want to make sure it's right. We/ you won't have a second chance," I said.

On Monday of the next week, Earl came into my office.

"Mel, is there any possibility that you can have your report done by tomorrow?

"I can have it done by tomorrow, but I can't guarantee the numbers, but I will guarantee the numbers on Wednesday."

"One day makes that much of a difference?"

"Yes, it does."

Earl looked at me hard and steady. I didn't back down.

"OK." he said and walked off.

That Wednesday, I am in Earl's office with his immediate staff of Directors, going over the Quality financials. Earl's meeting with the President is at 5:30 PM. I and six Directors all were going to wait in his office, just in case he needed anything. At 5:15, Earl left to go to the meeting. At about 6:30 PM, Earl walks back into the office where we all are waiting. All of us are trying to read his face. Earl looks at me and says;

"Mel, I think you are going to be in trouble."

And then with a smile, he says, "But not with me."

In summary, Finance had said that Quality was experiencing more financial problems than that which was being reported and there were some significant overruns not being addressed. The VP of Finance wanted to meet with the President and Earl to discuss the issues. In the meeting, Earl had an opportunity to present first, along with charts and numbers that myself and my team had prepared to support his position. Earl talked about the monthly meetings with his staff and the program QMs. He told the President how we review the numbers, the technical aspect of the program, identification of problems and corrective actions planned and taken. Earl also presented the progress chart that showed how we were reducing the overrun. Technically, the overrun was not Earl's fault, since that happened prior to his arrival. The fact that there was improvement, (projecting about five million) and heading in the right direction was significant.

After Earl presented, the President looked at the VP of Finance and asked him to show where the numbers were wrong. At about this time, the President's admin comes in and tells the President that he has a call from Corporate. The President excuses himself. The Finance VP takes this opportunity to call his staff, whom I'm sure were waiting in a room just as Earl's staff was waiting and asked them about the numbers Earl had presented. Just as the VP of Finance was getting off the phone, the President walks back into his office. He looks at the VP and asks;

"Well, are Earl's numbers right or is something wrong?"

The VP said that Earl's numbers were right, and that finance must have made an error somewhere.

"OK, let's move on to the next problem."

Earl presented once again. Once again, the President asked if Finance had an issue. Once again, the admin comes in and announces that a call has come in from Corporate (talk about timing). And, once again, the VP makes a call to his stand-by team. After a little longer wait this time, the President enters the room.

"Well, what's the verdict on this one?" the President asks.

The VP, with tongue in cheek, quietly said, "It appears that we don't have an issue with this program either."

"Well, I guess we can end this meeting." The president said.

So, when Earl said that I was going to be in trouble, he was acknowledging my line of reporting to Finance. Even though I was the Quality Business Manager, I reported into Finance, a matrix reporting system. So, essentially, I just made my boss, the VP of Finance look kinda foolish (this is the same VP that was instrumental in hiring me). True enough, the next day, one of the Finance Directors came to my office. This was significant in that he didn't ask me to come to his office.

He said, "Mel, the next time we have a financial meeting with the President involving Quality, I would like for you to have a pre-meeting with us. We need to reconcile both our numbers so that there are no surprises."

After that, there was small talk and then he left. You see, it didn't matter that they, Finance was the one who called the meeting. It didn't matter that they, Finance, who was putting Quality in a defensive position. And it was Finance who was trying to embarrass the Quality organization, and essentially throw me under the bus as the Business Manager. The fact that it ended up being Finance who was embarrassed was the reason the Finance Director was in my office. My assignment is to serve the Quality organization. The Finance organization just didn't count on me doing my job so well that it was to their embarrassment. But once again, there was no appreciation for the work that I had done. A familiar phrase came to mind:

"Civilians don't often appreciate nor reward leadership, innovation, or dedication. The service does and has recognized innate leadership in you; which, will not necessarily be so in the Civilian sector where politics and envy can come into play." Gen. Olds.

American Society for Quality Control (ASQC)

ASQC champions the cause of quality through a variety of fields and standards. ASQC provides support to a number of volunteer groups that develop and approve international and American National Standards. This includes the most widely known standards, such as ISO 9001, ISO 26000, and ISO 14001, as well as other standards and technical reports that apply quality management principles, tools and technology.

Once I became the Business Manager for Quality, Earl called me into his office to talk to me about ASQC of which he was the local chapter president.

"Well Mel, now that you are one of us (in the Quality organization) I would like for you to volunteer for some extra-curricular duties." Earl said.

"Volunteer? Yep, I've heard this one before."

"Of course, if you do volunteer, it will make your time and assignment easier here within Quality."

"OK, I know the drill, bend over and ..." I said as Earl began to laugh in earnest.

"No, Mel, I won't do that to you. You and I go way back, but I do need your help. I trust you and I know I can depend on you."

"OK, what is it that you need me to do?"

"I am the President of the local ASQC chapter, and I have to have meetings once a month. I have to find meeting sites, speakers, send out notices, encourage memberships, and a few other things to keep the chapter active and alive."

With a straight face I said, "If you are going to do all that, what do you need me for?"

Earl looked at me with a dumbfounded expression and then began laughing again.

"Alright Mel, I NEED YOU, to do those things in my behalf. And, in addition, I would like for you to be the treasurer as well. It will mean extra duty, but it will pay off for you and get you ingrained into Quality much faster. Until the staff sees you doing Quality 'stuff,' they will always think of you as an outsider. This way you'll be interacting with them more and will be talking about things that they are interested in, rather than finances, budgets, schedules, and the like."

"OK Earl, you know you are really straining this, 'We go way back thing.' And I think that is part of the problem, you know I don't mind challenges."

"Mel, we'll make a great team and I'm glad you're willing to work with me on this."

"I don't remember saying 'OK,' but 'OK,' I'll work with you on this. When do I start?

"How about now?"

"Now? OK let's spend some time to get me spun up on what ASQC is and what has been done in the chapter thus far this year."

"That's the beauty of this Mel, you get to start with a clean slate. We have to revive the chapter here in Orlando, so you get to do it your way."

"Oh great. Another start-up job, just what I needed."

I began working with Earl and doing the things that needed to be done to make ASQC a viable organization. Earl and I grew the membership from zero to about 200 members with about 30 – 60 attending the monthly meetings – dependent on the guest speaker and their topic.

During my membership in ASQC, I received a coveted award which was essentially an "MVP" award for the chapter. The head of ASQC came down to Orlando to present the award - The Henry DeZwart Award. A guy who considered himself a finance guy getting an award in Quality was something that they, ASQC leadership, just had not conceived; and was probably a first for the ASQC organization.

One day as I was sitting in my office, which is next to Earl's, Earl came in the room. This was unusual since Earl normally just buzzes and asks me to come into his office.

"Hi Mel do you have a moment?" Earl asks.

"Uh, sure. I can put aside what I am working on. What's up?"

"It's been three years now that I have been ASQC Chairman and I am thinking of stepping down."

"Gosh Earl, you are the face of ASQC here in Orlando, what do you think will happen once you step down?"

"I don't know. That's why I wanted to talk to you. You see, I believe if the organization has a chance to continue, only if you take the helm."

"Me? Why me? I am the most junior member of your staff, with the least amount of experience in Quality."

"What you say is true; however, you have shown yourself to be resilient, persistent, flexible, and a leader. Those qualities are going to be necessary to carry the chapter forward. Look Mel, I can sit here all day and tell you other things that you do well that have made me choose you to be my replacement."

With a smile, I sat back in my chair. "OK, start."

Earl sometimes does not have a sense of humor; however, I was OK if he chose not to receive my comment in the manner that it was given. I had what he wanted, me, so what could he do, get up and walk out? I was OK with that too.

With a brief hesitation, a gleam appeared in Earl's eyes, "Alright, alright, I know what you're trying to do, but it ain't gonna work. You're the guy I want."

We had about a three-month transition period when at the end of that time I officially became the ASQC President. Me, in Finance and the President of a local Quality Society chapter. I would not have guessed this in a million years when I left Los Angeles.

10th Wedding Anniversary – Cruising

In the summer of 1988 Renee and I met up with Ron and Josie, Mike and Beverlyn, who also got married the same month and year.

Before we left Los Angeles and moved to Orlando, we all had agreed to take a cruise for our 10th anniversary. Holding to our commitment, Renee and I drove down to Miami, to meet them at the Norwegian cruise line. It was only a three-day cruise, but since this was our first, we really didn't mind it being so short. After all, if it was a seven-day cruise, what could you do on a ship for all that time? (We have since taken several seven-day cruises and wished they all were longer.)

"Mel, do you think I'll get seasick on the cruise? I don't want my cruise to be ruined by being sick the whole time." Renee said.

"They have seasick tablets. We'll get you some when we get on board the ship," I said.

"OK. I really don't want to get sick."

We park the car and with suitcases in tow, made it through Customs, and walked up to the attendant at the check-in counter.

"Well, hello. Are you first time cruisers?" She said with a smile.

"That obvious, huh?" I said.

"Yeah. First timers have a certain glow about them that makes it easy to spot."

"We're meeting some friends for our 10th anniversary. We live in Orlando and they are flying in from Los Angeles. It will be their first time as well."

"Here are your boarding passes. Happy sailing."

"Thank you."

We got the passes and headed toward the ship. We marveled at the size of the ship as it lay at anchor. Renee stepped on the gangplank.

"Did you feel that?" as Renee holds her hand out as if she was balancing herself.

"Feel what?" I turn and stare at Renee in disbelief. Seeing how she had her hands out, and, wobbling.

"Feel the boat or gangplank, whatever. Did you feel it move?"

I look down between the ship and dock and see one-inch waves, not one foot but one inch. I humor her and say,

"Let's hurry and get on the ship, maybe you won't feel it as much. And besides, once we put our luggage in the room, we'll get you those seasick tablets."

"OK. Let's hurry then." Renee says.

As we entered the ship there was a porter there to help with luggage and guide us to our room. We opened the door to our cabin.

"Oh no, this is not going to work. We asked for a queen size bed, not two twins. We're gonna have to go back to check-in," I said.

The porter was very gracious and took us back to the ship entry point. We went back to the attendant that checked us in originally.

"Hi again. We requested a queen size bed and the cabin that we got has two twin size beds. If you recall, I mentioned that this is our 10th anniversary and twin-size beds won't work." I said with a crooked grin.

"Let's see what I can do. Huumm. I think I got something. Yep, I think this will work for you. Give this to the porter." As she gave us another slip of paper.

"OK. Thanks so much."

We go back and the same porter was there waiting. Since we were rather early, the porters were not very busy. He looks at the piece of paper.

"OK, follow me."

We follow him as he finds the nearest elevator. I didn't notice what floor he punched, but I was surprised at the sinking, and I literally mean sinking, feeling. We were going down. I got the feeling that we were below the waterline.

We no sooner stepped out of the elevator when I said, "This is not going to work either. This is worse than the other cabin. We need to go back to the check-in counter."

Again, the porter was very gracious as he escorted us back to the ship entry point. We went back to the attendant at the check-in counter.

"You know, I think you gave us a room that was below the waterline. It was very dark and drab. We never made it to the room; the hallway was bad enough," I said.

"Let me see the piece of paper."

I handed her the paper.

"The porter was taking us to this cabin." I read the cabin number to her. She began to laugh, almost hysterically.

"You just made my day," She said.

"So, what did I do to make your day?" I asked.

"You read the paper upside down. Read it this way. So, when you give it to the porter, make sure he reads it, this side up. Oh boy, that was a good one. I'll be going on my break soon, thanks for the story. We get prizes if we can come up with the best story for first timers. I think I'll get the prize this week. Enjoy your anniversary."

We went back to our porter (we felt like we could claim ownership by now). He looked at us with a quizzical expression as is in, 'Now what?' I gave him the same piece of paper.

He looked at the paper and said, "So, what is different?"

"Turn it upside down," I said.

Once he turned the paper, a huge grin came across his face.

"Follow me." He beamed.

We went to the same elevator, but this time I felt that we were resisting gravity, not going with it. It didn't hurt that I made it a point to see what floor he pushed. When I saw the floor he pushed, a smile came across my face. When the elevator doors opened, it opened unto a private suite of eight cabins. The smile never left the porter's face as he opened the door to the cabin. The cabin itself was a suite. It had a sitting area, a bedroom, a shower, and a bathtub. Nice. It turned out to be one of the owner's cabins. We tipped the porter handsomely, and praised God for favor.

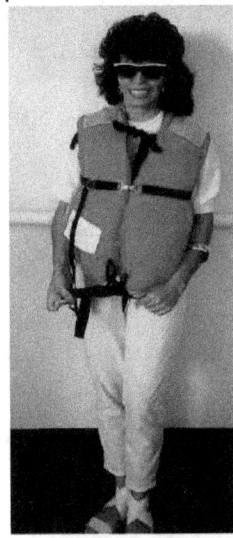

"Let's go get those seasick pills, then we can unpack. I'm sure they'll need a couple of hours to begin working, so let's give them a head start," I said.

We went to the medical station and got a couple of seasick pills. I am OK so I didn't bother to get any for me. When we got back to the room, Renee took one of the seasick pills. Even after taking one of the pills, Renee was starting to feel a little woozy. After we un-packed, Renee really began to feel uncomfortable.

"Why don't you lay down and I'll see if I can find Ron and Josie. I'll be back."

It took me about 45 minutes to find Ron and Josie. Meanwhile, unbeknownst to me, Renee took another seasick pill. Ron and Josie came back with me to our room.

"Wow, how did you guys' rate rooms up here?" Ron asked.

"Wait until we get inside then I'll tell you the whole story," I said.

"Wait here for a moment, let me make sure Renee is dressed."

"OK, no problem. If not, just tell my sister she needs to hurry up and get dressed, and not leave her sister and brother out here in the cold." Ron said.

I laughed and entered the cabin. Renee was presentable.

"Ron and Josie are outside waiting to see you. Are you OK to talk?"

"Suuure" Renee said.

I hesitated a moment after hearing how she responded.

"I'll get them."

"Rooon aaannnd Joooosie, it is soooo niiiice tooo see yoooou. Wheeen diiiid yooooou coooome iiinnn?"

Ron and Josie both looked at me at the same time. Renee was talking really slow and dragging her words out.

29

"Mel, brother, can I speak to you outside?" It was more of a statement than a question.

I couldn't help but chuckle as I knew what Ron wanted to ask me.

"Now I know it has been a few years since we have seen each other, but I'm concerned about my sister. Is she OK? She's not on drugs or anything is she? She's talking really slow."

With what Ron said, I began to laugh in earnest.

"Now this is no laughing matter. I'm really concerned." Ron said.

"Ron, she is OK. She took a seasick pill and I guess it has just made her really drowsy. Let's find out if she took anything else."

As we entered back into the cabin, Josie turned around to look at us with a very, very concerned look.

"Renee, did you take any other medication with that seasick pill?" I asked.

"Nooo. The oooone waaaasn't wooooorking tooo weeeell sooo I tooook aaanooother oooone. Whyyy?" She commented.

"Do you realize that you are talking very slowly?"

"Noooo. I sooound fiiine tooo meee."

With the mystery solved, we all relaxed and laughed with and about Renee and her speech pattern.

We met up with Mike and Beverlyn later that evening, and, we found out that three other couples associated with Ron and Josie had also made the trip. Fortunately, Renee's speech did improve by the time we met the other couples.

The second night out, we were able to gain access to the Captain's Boardroom where all of us reaffirmed our wedding vows and played a game called Win, Lose, or Draw. It was the guys against the gals. Don't remember all the details in playing the game except that drawing an object, with minimal  time, is crucial. It was amazing. Us guys would draw something that at least resembled the real thing. It may have taken a little longer but we would get the correct answer. The ladies, it was like, well, totally incomprehensible. One of the girls drew something that was like an elongated "S" with a cross hatch.

The ladies cried out, "It's a woman putting on lipstick."

"Huh?" All the guys responded.

The whole game went on in this manner. The ladies would draw something that us guys didn't have a clue. Needless to say, they won the game that night.

The next day we docked at a private island where the cruise line prepared a Bar B Que lunch; and, wouldn't you know it, they had a Limbo contest. As we left the island, I was given the official title as "Limbo King." Yep, I won the contest. Oh yeah, I was runner-up in the Men's division of "Best Legs." I think everyone was getting out of their comfort zone, and was just enjoying the ride.

During the whole trip I took advantage of the morning, mid-morning, lunch, late afternoon, dinner eating times, and oh, almost forgot, the midnight breakfast times. The group looked at me and marveled that it looked as if I was not putting on any pounds. In actuality, I may have gained one or two pounds, but not the multiples as they imagined.

The cruise ended too quickly for all of us.

One of our Own

Black individuals at Martin Marietta/ Lockheed Martin comprise about 5% of their salary/ managerial staff. Because of this low percentage, I believe Black managers or those in Salary positions are under greater scrutiny than their White counterparts. This observation and experience heightened my awareness of the disparate expectations and acceptance of Black employees. So whenever possible I would attempt to assist other Black employees if I observe behavior that is counter-productive. Many Black employees knew this and often commented about their appreciation and have said, "You have stuck your neck out when others won't give the time of day."

Mind you, I had a reputation at Martin that I will work with anyone; and turn them into a better performer. I didn't do reverse discrimination. It just is that I knew some Black individuals needed a little help in threading the political waters in the workplace.

One day, after hours, at work, I encountered a young lady that I had worked with before in Finance. This lady is Black and has excellent potential. We were near my office so I asked her if she wouldn't mind coming to my office to get out of the hallway so that I may speak with her. She agreed, so we entered my office, however, I kept the door open just so there wouldn't be any confusion on my intent.

"Brenda, I would like to share something with you. It may prove to be helpful to you."

"Sure. What is it? Brenda said.

"I am in a lot of meetings and when I hear your name come up, this is what I hear, 'She's a great worker, BUT, you have to be careful around her." "She's excellent in what she does, But. . . " or, "She knows her stuff, BUT . . . " "Brenda, I just want to be helpful because I doubt that anyone will tell you what people are saying about you. I think you have a great career, just got to clean up the 'BUTS.' If I can help you with that, I don't mind."

We talked for a few minutes after that.

Then Brenda said, "Is there anything else you want to share with me?"

"No. Only to say, if I can help, let me know."

With that, Brenda left my office.

The following day I am in my office when the phone rings.

"Hi Mel, this is Sharon."

"Hi Sharon, what do I owe the pleasure of this call?"

"Well Mel, this one isn't so pleasant."

"OK, soooo... what's the matter?"

"Can you come to the EEO office?"

"Now?"

"If you can."

"Sure, give me about 10 minutes."

The EEO is the Equal Employment Opportunity office. The office handles any discrimination or harassment claims. Sharon herself is a Black female that is aware of many instances where I have taken a Black employee "under my wings" so to speak, to help them navigate a troubling storm in the workplace. She is also acquainted with the many challenges that I have personally faced to be successful within the Lockheed Martin environment.

"Hi Sharon, What's up?"

"I have a complaint against you from a female employee name Brenda."

"Brenda. That is strange. I spoke with her last night about how she is viewed by others within the company; and, that I was willing to help her work through what could be a negative perception of her. What did she say that I said?"

"Knowing you Mel, what you just said does not surprise me. However, I have to go on record that I spoke with you."

"You know Sharon, I don't have to help anyone; and, you know the number of people I have helped since I have been at this company."

"I know Mel, which is why I was so reluctant to call you. I know you only want to help."

"OK. That's it. I won't stick my neck out anymore. I'm done."

"Mel, I don't want you to stop what you are doing because of one person. You have helped too many people to let one person stop you. As I said, I had to talk to you for the record, but that is all I intend to do. We don't have enough managers here that are willing to help others, so

I don't want to lose one that is doing so; and, if I might say, a fine job at that."

"Boy, what a bum deal when one of our own does this to you. No one else would have told her what I said to her, or if they did, it would not have been to help. OK Sharon, I won't stop, but believe me, I will not be as generous in my willingness to help."

"Mel, as long as you won't stop trying to help, that's all that I can ask."

"Well, I guess we'll have to see what the future holds."

For months following, when Brenda's name came up in meetings, the "But" qualifier was still present. I often thought, if she only knew.

Another Black-on-Black incident came up one day as I was going to lunch. I was talking to one of the "brothers" as we were walking to lunch.

"Did you see that Magic game last night? Shaquille was just awesome. He gets better every year. And Penney is even looking better." Butch said.

"Yeah, I'm all for the Magic until they play the Lakers... gotta vote for the home team," I said.

"Oh, I didn't know you were from Los Angeles, how long have you been in Orlando?"

"Moved here in April of '85. Family came out later that year. Haven't really given any thought of moving back to L.A. though. Still call it home, but I like Orlando better. "
At about this time we had just arrived at the cafeteria doors.

"You going to lunch now." Butch asked.

"Yeah, going to eat with the big guys."

"Why don't you ever come and sit with us?"

"Honestly Butch, I think where and how you guys eat lunch sets a bad example. You isolate yourselves, as if you got a clique or something going. Ever hear of Rosa Parks?"

"No, why?"

"Well, she was the one that really started the Civil Rights movement."

"Oh, was she the one that didn't want to sit in the back of the bus?"

"That's her. So, you have heard about what she did, you just didn't know the name. Fair enough. When I go in the cafeteria, and I see all you Black folks sitting together, and not mingling, I can't help but to think, 'What a setback.' After all the years and all the lives lost to integrate, you and the others are segregating yourselves, voluntarily. Do you realize the handicap that places upon you and the others? The folks that run this place already have difficulty in relating to us, you're not helping to change that. How are they going to know us, you, if you, we, don't take time to interact with them? I don't sit with any particular group, but I do go to the Executive cafeteria, just so they can see a Black face sitting amongst them. After all, there are not many of us black managers in management in this company, and many times I am the only Black manager in the Executive cafeteria.

Have you ever heard about 'Crabology?' People hunting for crabs use an open bucket to put the crabs in when the crabs are caught. There is no fear about the crabs crawling out and getting away. When one crab gains a foothold on the side of the bucket, invariably, another crab will reach up and pull it back into the bucket. I often think this is analogous of the Black social interaction. When one 'person of color' begins to ascend or become, what is considered, successful, there always seems to be those that want to pull them back down. It is unfortunate that Blacks are themselves their own police or watchdog. Watching to make sure some uppity character doesn't try to escape. It is *Uncommon* for Blacks to realize that to be successful, at times, you have to think 'White.' This doesn't mean a Black person has to give up their Black roots or identity. Won't happen. One look and the secret is out. What it does mean is to do what so many other ethnic groups have done, support one another.

In most ethnic centers, money will circulate or exchange hands within the community about six or seven times before it leaves the community. In a Black community, it may circulate twice before it leaves. Most Blacks will leave their neighborhood to patronize a similar business in another part of town rather than support a Black owned business in their own community.

It also means not congregating in groups of three or more. Whenever that happens, the "establishment" becomes uneasy. For this reason, it is not good to join the 'Black' table for lunch. In many ways it is self-imposed segregation; and, a person can miss out on the latest happenings within the company since many Blacks are not in positions to 'know.' I'm trying to let them see that you and I have the same concerns, desires, and most importantly, the ability to communicate on their level. You don't know how many times, while sitting at lunch, one of the Directors or VPs, will say, 'Mel, you are very articulate. You express yourself very well.' They don't know that to me, when they say that I am "articulate" that it is an insult. You ever hear them say that about any other ethnic group? It is as if they are surprised that I can talk. Still, it is the reason why I go. I'm trying to break down barriers, stereotypes, prejudices, or whatever else that puts us at a disadvantage. Staying segregated is not going to help our cause."

"Wow. Didn't know I was going to push a hot button."

"Yeah, maybe it is a hot button. The problem is I have been faced with unspoken prejudices, unfair acts, and who knows what else, just because I'm a little different. Why are there so few Black managers in the company? Not just this company, but here in the U.S.? We got to expose ourselves. We need to go out amongst them, interact with them; then I believe we will begin to see more Black faces in management."

"Mel, you gave me a lot to think about. But not now. I'm going to go and sit with my brothas and sistas today."

I smiled and said, "OK, I'll keep trying to pioneer a way for you and your brothas and sistas. See ya later."

I hope, in the near future; more and more Black individuals will wise up and dare to be "Uncommon."

Quality Assurance
Government Audit

One of the reasons that Earl was at Martin Marietta was due to a very poor performance during a government audit. The audit was so bad that the audit team stop writing discrepancies halfway through the audit cycle, and just declared the audit a failure. Well, Earl and his new team, including myself, were committed to not having a poor or lackluster performance on the upcoming audit. We spent months getting the company in shape for the audit. As well as having my own area of responsibility "Cost of Quality," I was put in charge of the "care and feeding" of the audit team. We set aside a special area for the auditors. They each had their own desk, supplied with pencils, pens, paper, paper clips, etc. The area had its own conference room as well as a small cubicle for coffee and snacks. They were very impressed with the accommodations and said so at the opening meeting.

The auditors conducted their audit primarily in pairs and there were about 30 auditors in total. The audit was to last a week. Prior to the start of the audit, a tour of the facility was scheduled. The Marietta facility in Orlando is quite large (see **Fig 3-2**). Earl's immediate staff members were assigned to give the initial tour of the facility. Earl and I partnered and had about eight of the audit team, including the most senior members.

We were about an hour into the tour when we walked into the Shipping & Receiving Department. The dress of the day (circa 1987) was a business suit with tie. This was a common dress for office personnel. As we walked into the large bay where most of the shipping and receiving was done, we heard this loud female voice proclaim,

"Mel, first time I've seen you with clothes on! Oh, I mean, you're all dressed up and you look different. I mean you always had clothes on. . ."

The lady turned and walked away. She was too embarrassed to stay in the area. It was a classic speak before thinking moment. After she realized what she said, she tried to cover it up, making it worse. It was the highlight of the day for
the Government audit team. I tried to explain that she was referring to our company sponsored softball team, of which we both participated. Previously she had only seen me in shorts and T-shirt, but that didn't matter. What was done was done. That afternoon, the audit team began auditing in earnest, but occasionally after we finished an area, one of them would say, "Hey Mel, you got time to go get dressed."

The following day I got a page (like a text message) to report to a Parts Holding area. As I was going, I encountered Earl, who had gotten a similar page. We walked into the area and were greeted by about five QMs, all in a concerned conversation. For some reason, this particular area had been omitted from the clean-up that had been going on for the last few months. Parts had components and tags missing, were miss-located, the whole area was just in dis-array.

Earl looked at me and asked, "When is this area scheduled to be audited?"

I checked the schedule.

"It is scheduled for just after lunch tomorrow, and I am on duty to escort the Government team responsible for the audit," I said.

Fast Forward - The next day, at the usual morning audit meeting, the senior management team was at the briefing; however, today, the Company President decided to attend the briefing as well. The lead auditor came to the podium, looked out at the Martin staff and said,

"It's amazing. What a difference. We are looking extremely hard, and the comparison to our last audit is like night and day. If this trend continues, we may end our audit a day early."

Now we didn't know what the Lead auditor would say that following morning. What we did know was that the shape that this area was in was putting the whole audit in jeopardy. There was no way we were going to get this area cleaned up in time. Knowing that it would not pass mustard, we put all our energies into making it look presentable. It was neat, it was spotless. Fortunately, the adjacent and similar area had been cleaned up and was prepared for audit. This other area was ready to go and figured prominently in our strategy. We spent a little extra time to really make this other area look good.

The next day, I picked up the audit team and took them on their morning route. All the areas were consistently above average, so the audit team was in a fairly good mood. We broke for lunch. I took the opportunity to get with Earl one more time, prior to our venture into the "Dooms Den" as we started calling the one area.

"You know Earl, I wouldn't mind if you pulled rank at any time if you want to lead the audit team" I said.

"No thanks. It would be best if I stayed as the appeal authority." He said with a big grin.

"Yea, right." I said sarcastically.

At one o'clock, I went to get the audit team. By now, the dialog between us was cordial, but respectful, so I'm sure to them the walk to the audit area seemed pleasant. Me, I felt like I was walking the "Green Mile." As we got to the area, the Dooms Den was the first room that we encountered. The audit team was about to walk in, when I said,

"The other room over there has more parts, will probably take longer to complete, and besides, we can check this one on the way out."

They looked at one another and shrugged their shoulders.

"OK," they said.

The team went to the other room where they spent most of the afternoon. By the time they finished that one room, and found not one discrepancy, the day was mostly spent. As we walked out of the room, back down the hallway, we passed the Dooms Den. One of our Quality guys said,

"Are you going to check this room?"

I could have killed him, and probably would have, until the audit team lead, said,

"You guys have been doing so well and the room we just left was spotless. I think we would be wasting our time here. I would rather go to another area."

With that, I thanked the Lord and under my breath said, "Hallelujah," as we walked away. Disaster averted. I quietly asked one of the Quality Managers walking with us to go to Earl to let him know we were out of the area...safely.

The audit did end a day early. The lead Government auditor was extremely surprised of the low number of findings and the number of major areas of "No Findings." One of those areas was my responsibility, "Cost of Quality." The lead auditor was so impressed that he said that he was going to recommend that the Company participate in a new Government program called "Contractor Performance Certification Program" (CPCP) or (CP) squared. This Quality Excellence Program would reduce the number of daily routine Government audits and the frequency of major audits. A reduction in either of these audits would translate to a significant cost savings to the company. This is the report that was released by the local newspaper, "...the government auditors had been at the Sand Lake Road plant for two weeks investigating several hundred pieces of hardware. As a result of its performance, Missile Systems has become only the second company to qualify for the command's contractor performance certification program. The Army said that Martin's score was the highest it had awarded in the four years since the program began."

Prime Rib Lunch

Myself, acting as the Company coordinator, and my government counterpart took six months and an untold number of man-hours to lay the ground work to initiate the kick-off of an 18-month Government Quality program. The company was going to recognize the significance of this event by giving all 16,000 employees a free, prime rib lunch, have several generals from the Redstone Arsenal attend, invite corporate staffers, invite the county mayor, and many other politicians. The ceremony was to occur on the front lawn just in front of the seven-story tower. (This whole process repeated itself, 20 months later, as the company was rewarded by being acknowledge as a Quality Excellence or CPCP participant.) My initial role as coordinator transitioned into Program Manager. For the next 18 months, in addition to my regular duties, managing a staff of 26, maintaining our Cost of Quality program, being the editor of a new Quality newspaper, coordinating any audits, and implementing a new "Total Quality Management" program for the company, I had to coordinate and report to the Government our quality performance. This reporting was done via a tracking report, providing on-going stats on how well we were doing on daily and spontaneous audits.

Once again, do you think appreciation was expressed for the role I played to coordinate and program manage the CPCP program? Nope, nada. However, my government counterpart, who happened to be Black, received a bonus and a promotion for his efforts in helping to make this program a reality. Most of the work was on my end. There was no recognition of having no findings in my area of Cost of Quality, no recognition for coordinating both ceremonies, no recognition for heading up the 18-month program that resulted in multi-million-dollar savings for the company in hours and dollars. I knew a many of other managers that did half of what I did and received recognition and bonus dollars. I just didn't understand. The company had a great opportunity to show impartiality, to act in a non-prejudicial way yet choose not to. No one could deny the work that I had put into the Quality Excellence

Program nor the success of the program. But again, there was neither recognition nor reward but, "**A Glass Unbroken**." That's why it is so puzzling to me when I hear that companies can't find Black individuals to promote or to put in senior management. My effort was visible to the Government, other corporations, and especially to my own company, Martin Marietta (now, Lockheed Martin). ***"Civilians don't often appreciate nor reward leadership, innovation, or dedication. The service does and has recognized innate leadership in you; which, will not necessarily be so in the civilian sector where politics and envy can come into play." Gen. Olds***.

Total Quality Management

In addition to being the Business Manager for the Quality Organization, Earl recognized my organizational skills and would often have me lead any new venture. One of these ventures was Total Quality Management (TQM). The idea was to make quality such a common-place item in all that we do that it becomes second nature. Many businesses have based their success on "quality" production. They would have mottos such as "Quality First," "Build it Right the First Time," or "Zero Defects," plus others. A person would think that a company would welcome the idea of building a quality product; and, Lockheed Martin did. However, there was a little factor that would come into play that could pose a huge hindrance, the rivalry between Quality and Engineering. Engineers often had a big ego and their motto could be summed up in "I designed it, you build it." It didn't matter if their design could have been made simpler for manufacturing or not. For instance, at Hughes, there was one sub assembly that had small indicator lights that were hard-wired in the unit. When a light went out, 1) the sub-assembly had to be removed from the chassis, 2) the back panel removed, and then 3) with a soldering iron, the burnt-out bulb was removed. Replacing the bulb was done in reverse order. The best thing would have been for the bulb to be removed from the front, by simply screwing it out, and screwing in the replacement bulb. The engineers here were no different. So, I not only had to introduce a concept that the Quality organization was always touting, "Build it/ Design it Right the First Time," but I had to get the Engineering organization to accept a change in their culture without feeling that "they lost."

I started with an advertising blitz. With the help of a graphic artist, I designed a TQM logo that would be posted throughout the company (to my amazement, I visited a Lockheed Martin facility 15 years later and saw the same logo on the walls).

The paragraph following the Management Club article can be found on the Lockheed Martin website as of December 2012. The paragraph summarizes the results of the processes in which I was lead, TQM, ISO 9001, Baldrige Award, and the Army's Quality Certification Program. My efforts brought a fundamental change in the way the company did business, yet once again, I was never recognized by the company for the leadership or work performed. Ironically, the company's Management Club did recognize my efforts in the extremely successful TQM campaign. I was featured in their 1990 Newsletter, in their "Role of Honor" section. The write-up was as follows:

> *Mel was involved in planning, developing, and implementing TQM for Group and Missile Systems. His efforts, as well as his team members, will result in our company being recognized in the Contractor Performance Certification Program and will be the first Martin Marietta Corporation facility to achieve this honor. Mel and his wife Renee have arranged, coordinated, and conducted the popular photographic sessions for the past three Dinner Dances.*

I appreciated the recognition; however, they still didn't get it right. Truly, I was "involved" in planning, but I was also the "leader" in the planning, developing, and implementation of TQM.

While at the dinner, we were sitting eight to a table, when I had to leave to coordinate the photo shoot. A Vice-president that knew me quite well was also at the table, sitting next to Renee. The VP was with his wife but would occasionally lean over and say something to Renee. That evening, on the way home, Renee told me what the VP had said when I left to check on the photo shoot.

She said the VP told her, "You know if Mel wasn't Black, and played golf, he'd be a VP by now."

Imagine that.

Being Black I had no control of; and, I wasn't going to sacrifice my time or weekends with Renee, Aaron, Dez, and Darien to be a VP, playing golf, requiring more time away from home.

As you look at the pyramid below, you can see that TQM was the base that set the company on course to win other Quality awards.

The 12/12 Website reads as follows:

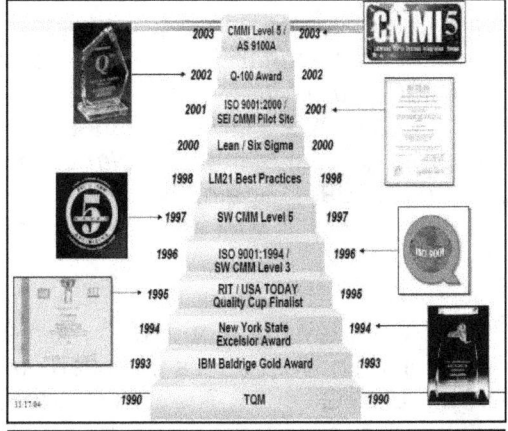

From Lockheed Martin's Website – 12/12

As the result of a government audit in 1985, Martin Marietta Electronics and Missiles (E&M) developed a Total Quality Management (TQM) plan that has evolved into today's Embedded Quality Systems Plan. This plan focuses on those system elements and processes required to provide assurance that products and services meet the requirements of the Customer. The program has been very successful and since 1989, there have been no government audit deficiencies.

Lockheed Martin previously had the typical hidden factory where products were reworked to meet the requirements. Problems causing non-conformances were never addressed other than with band-aid style quick fixes. Quality was inspected-in instead of Lockheed Martin developing quality processes, resulting in millions of dollars' worth of scrap. The 1985 audit identified deficiencies that served to alert Lockheed Martin that action must be taken to correct the situation immediately. The key elements of Embedded Quality Systems Plan address those areas highlighted during the audit and include:

- *Achieving ISO 9001 registration*
- *Implementing Production Process Validation*
- *Developing and implementing a system audit program*
- *Establishing a Preventive Action Board*
- *Achieving Software Engineering Institute Level 3 certification*
- *Developing Best Practices Guidelines*

ISO 9001 certification was received in December 1994 (Participated in this effort and lead one of several teams to a successful contribution). *The assessment, performed by BSI-QA, gave Lockheed Martin Electronics & Missiles international registration and allowed the company to compete worldwide. This certification has prompted Lockheed Martin to take an innovative look at processes and practices instead of the MIL-Q-9858A way.*

Following TQM implementation, I was tasked to head up the charge to receive the *Malcolm Baldrige Award.* We were awarded this honor in 1993. Again, there was no recognition by Lockheed Martin for the work I did in successfully orchestrating this effort.

The Life Giver

One day I responded to a city-wide call from an organization that was planning to put on a Christian play. The name of the play was called "The Life Giver." They needed volunteers in many areas, actors, actresses, musicians, stagehands, lighting, sound, etc. The play was scheduled to be held at the Tupperware Headquarters in their 3000-seat auditorium with an ultimate cast of about 90 individuals. The props were full size and moveable. This facility is located about 40 minutes west of Orlando. I showed up at the check-in station where I was asked, in what area was I interested. Although I had video production and sound board experience, somehow, I wasn't led to say so. I think I got assigned to a "general" category and "next" was quickly announced. That evening I found myself, along with about 15 others, moving things around the stage and removing what could be cleared. One item of significance was a Grand Piano. It had to be taken off the stage and put down in the orchestra pit, manually. The guys moving the piano had just gotten started when I came upon the scene. What I saw was a disaster in the making. I could just picture this Grand Piano in the pit, broken into a thousand pieces. I ran over to the guys.

"Guys, guys, wait a minute! Let's set the piano down for just a minute. Let's rehearse what we are going to do and who is going to do what before we attempt to lower the piano in the pit. I'm sure none of us have ever worked together, and I'm also sure none of us want to be the one paying for this thing."

At first there was silence, then a "Sounds good to me,"

"Yea, would hate to drop this thing," someone said.

"Wouldn't hurt to give it some thought," another said.

With that, I lead the discussion and planning for the move until we were comfortable with what everyone had to do. We got the piano in the pit. In one piece. The rest of the moving was uneventful.

The next day I got a call at work and was asked if I would come to Tupperware early and speak with the Assistant Director (AD) of the play.

I met the AD back at the Tupperware auditorium that afternoon, right after work.

He said, "Mel, Tom (the Director) and I saw what happened last night. We were extremely concerned about the Grand Piano and was about to say something when you came on the scene. When you showed up, we both looked at each other and said, 'Let's see what happens.' Needless to say, we were extremely impressed, which is why I am talking to you now. You see, the stage crew chief we've had for years is unable to join us this year. We were in a quandary as to what we were going to do about that position until we saw you in action last night. You probably didn't give it a second thought; however, Tom and I both thought the same thing at the same time. 'This guy will work. He took control of a very questionable situation and exhibited leadership capabilities with guys he didn't know. So here I am, asking if you wouldn't mind taking the lead position and head up the Stage Crew?"

Boy, was I shocked. It goes to show you; you never know who's watching. I asked what it would entail such as what hours, responsibility and the number of people involved. After we talked, I told him that I thought I would give it a try. I also told him that my feelings would not be hurt if at any time he wanted to put someone else in the position. It is often said that God does not let us see the future, because if He did, we would lack the courage to accept it. The future I faced with this play was not life threatening. However, if someone came to me that day and said, "How would you like to be the Stage Manager for a Broadway play?" This was the equivalent and I am sure most people would not want to be a stage manager for a Broadway Play with a day's notice.

About the Play

The play was primarily a musical. Tom wrote the play and wrote many of the songs. The singers had excellent voices and really brought the play to life. The props for this play were life size, huge. The props primarily looked like houses, inns, castles, boats, even the Garden of Gesemene and Golgotha, the hill of the crucifixion, were places in which a fairly large group could walk. They were large enough that people were either on them or in them. Our challenge was to move these monsters in and out of position multiple of times, in a timely fashion. We had gotten all of the props on a Tuesday. Opening night was that coming Friday. Thursday night, we were going through rehearsal and were stuck on one scene change. It was the "Triumphant Entry" to the Upper Room. The first time we did the transition it took 21 minutes. Tom stopped everybody.

"We got to get the time down to three minutes." Tom said looking at the Stage Crew.

Those of us on the stage crew looked at each other, shrugged our shoulders.

"We'll see what we can do," we said.

We took some time to talk it over, rearranged and sat the staging for the next attempt.

"Let's try it again," I said.

This time we got it down to 13 minutes. Still wasn't quick enough. Tom was very appreciative of the reduction in time but he knew he couldn't live with a 13-minute scene change.

"What are we going to do?" Tom said out of exasperation.

"Sing another song." The person playing Jesus jokingly responded.

That comment was the tension breaker. I mentioned to Tom that it would be great if the whole cast got involved in trying to figure out how we can reduce the time. What resulted was phenomenal. Tom in fact did write another song to put in, however, all we needed was the three extra minutes for a total of six minutes for the change-over. This was less than half of the 13 minutes and out of the park from the 21. The way that we were able to accomplish this feat was in-fact, by getting the cast members involved. Previously, only the stage crew moved any and every prop, even the smallest item such as a vase or a piece of fruit. What we did was to assign a prop to every cast member. No one was to leave the stage without something in their hand.

The AD later commented. "When I saw this transition take place for the first time it was like a whirlwind. Everybody running everywhere things all over the place, then suddenly, everything was gone, and then there was calm. Amazing."

42 Hours

Ever watch the program "24 Hours?" Where they show what happens in a day. Well, I will take you on a quick journey of 42 hours. Thursday morning, the day before opening night of The Life Giver, I got up at 6:00 AM, got dressed and went to work. By 6:00 PM (12 hours later) I was at the Tupperware facility going through rehearsal. We continued rehearsal until 4:00 AM Friday morning (22 hours). Even at that, we never got through every scene. At 4:00 AM, Tom called everyone together and asked the question,

"Do we cancel tonight's performance?"

There was some discussion amongst the cast members, then Tom asked me,

"Can the Stage Crew do it, not having gone through all the scenes?"

Of course, I had been pondering this same question, so when he asked, I knew what I was going to say.

"True, none of us have gone through every scene. But what is most important, the scenes or the person of Jesus Christ? The props that we have here can only be rivaled by Hollywood, so I suspect the audience will be in awe of what they do see. Only we will know if we don't do something or leave a prop off or put it in the wrong place. Also, it is the first night and I believe people will be more forgiving on the first night than at any other time. Besides, we can call it our first full dress rehearsal."

With that last comment, everyone laughed and began nodding their head in agreement.

"Well then, I'll see everyone here at 5:00."

"Five, that's only a half hour from now," someone said jokingly.

I think everyone was giddy about this time.

"Uh, 5:00 PM tonight, it'll give you plenty of time to get dressed." Tom said.

By the time I left the Tupperware facility and got home it was 6:00 AM (24 hours). We didn't have cell phones, so there wasn't any way that I could notify Renee and let her know that I was still at rehearsal. I tried to tip toe in the room, but Renee was up. She said she woke up as soon as she heard the garage door opening. With her being awake, I gave up all pretenses of being quiet. I ran in the bathroom, took a shower, performed my ablutions, went to the closet and got a suit, shirt, tie and shoes. I was ready in about 15 minutes. I kissed Renee and went to work.

We had a couple of meetings that morning, went on the shop floor, and essentially stayed active. I was glad that it was a busy day, but I didn't look forward to a 3:00 PM meeting that afternoon. That meeting could be a killer, with my lack of sleep and all. As it approached 3:00 PM (33 hours), a group of us began walking to Earl's office for the meeting. Just as we were about to get into the elevator, Earl asked if I would wait a moment as he wanted to ask me a question. Now I had been with Earl, the Quality Director, most of the day, so I thought it strange that he wanted to speak to me now.

"Mel, are you OK?"

"Yes. Why."

"Well, I noticed earlier today that you did something strange. I mean, you always dress so well, impeccably so, that I had to look several times before I believed what I saw."

By now, Earl really got my attention.

"What are you talking about? I'm wearing a suit, got a tie on and I didn't forget my shirt."

"Well, you wanna look at your shoes? One is black and the other is blue."

Earl must have seen the consternation on my face and then jokingly said,

"I bet you got another pair at home just like those?"

Just think, I had been going the whole day with one black and one blue shoe. In the dark, in my haste, I grabbed the wrong color shoe, and I didn't know it. Actually, they were boots, both of the same style, just different color. I started re-living my day trying to think if I noticed anybody looking down at my feet, or if they were acting strangely. What the heck, what is done is done. Moreover, I knew if I told Earl not to tell anyone, everyone he would tell. So, I laughed it off.

"I'll wear the other pair next Monday."

With that, we got into the elevator.

I made it through the meeting and left at 4:00 PM. Earl knew I had to leave early and why I had to leave. I got Earl's attention; he acknowledged and nodded his head. I got up walked to the door and just as I was about to walk out, Earl said,

"We'll see that other pair next week."

I closed the door. I don't know what was said after I closed the door, but I figure, since I was gone, they couldn't confirm the fact, therefore I could always plead denial. I arrived at Tupperware at a little before 5:00 PM, changed clothes and began prepping the stage. When 6:00 PM came, I had a momentary thought of being awake for 36 hours without sleep. We had a really nice crowd for an opening night. We had some glitches as well; however, there was probably only one that the crowd would have noticed. We didn't have time to place rocks in front of one the risers before the curtain opened, so the framework was exposed. Still, at the end of the show we got a standing ovation. Whew!

Tom was very happy for the way the performance went and expressed his appreciation once again to the cast and crew. By the time we got everything stowed and prepped for the next day performance it was just after midnight (42 hours). The matinee performance began at 3:00 PM, so I had to be back by 1:00 PM that same day and be ready to do it all over again by 7:30 PM. The play ran for nine days and every showing received a standing ovation. I was whipped. We had a lot of people commenting about the life-size props and the fact that the stage was changed so quickly, even with the large props. We had our mishaps, such as a Roman soldier falling into the orchestra pit and the character of Jesus actually being hit by one of the guards and losing consciousness.

Tom really appreciated the work that the Stage Crew did. So much so that during the curtain call he gave us a one-minute opportunity to recreate a scene. It was an open curtain, so the audience could see what we were doing, and the Director began counting down from 30 to

get the audience involved.

They loved it. I had the last piece to be put in place. One time the Director saw that we were a little behind and he purposely repeated one of the numbers. The audience wouldn't have it. The audience picked up the count without the overlap and got louder and louder. They were really into it. We saw that we were not going to get any grace or mercy, so we really had to pick up the tempo. 3...2.... The fountain was in my hand, the final piece. I was not going to make it. Without hesitation,

and obviously without forethought, the crowd, as one, stretched out the last number for about two seconds until I dropped the fountain in place. The audience began to whoop and holler like crazy. That was what it was all about. It made the long hours, the mismatched shoes, the sleepless days all worth it. Tom couldn't thank the crew enough. He got a lot of compliments from the audience about the staging and the Stage Crew and even the cast members themselves made mention of the Stage Crew. A couple of weeks after the play, Tom and his wife took Renee and I out to dinner to show his appreciation for my work on the Stage Crew and what he said was a "Phenomenal act."

In Memory of: Tom Russell: **30 Sep 1946 – 3 Nov 2010**

Quality Assurance
A Freeze on Hiring

After one of the financial meetings within the financial organization, I had privy to attend, I came back to my office to review staffing of the Quality organization. We had over 900 personnel on the books. After the review, I made up my mind that I had to meet with Earl and convince him to freeze all hiring. As I sat across from him and gave my report, he asked,

"Why do you want to freeze hiring when all other organizations, especially manufacturing, is hiring?"

"I believe within 12 – 14 months, the company will experience a downturn and will begin laying people off. I saw the company financials and I don't see how we can continue to hire, knowing what's coming."

"Mel, how is it that you are the only one seeing this?"

"Because I care. The other day, while sitting in the Executive Lunchroom, I heard the Manufacturing VP brag about hiring people for a year, and then as work decreases, lay them off. Earl, who here in Orlando would pass up an opportunity to work with Martin Marietta? Here it is, the VP bragging about hiring folks, taking them away from perhaps long-term employment, only to lay them off within a year. That to me is being heartless. If you want to follow manufacturing, then that is what will happen. We will bring people on for a year and then lay them off. If we freeze hiring, except for critical skills, let attrition occur, we can be at an acceptable staffing level when the layoffs begin. Besides, Christmas is coming up, we can do overtime where extra staffing is needed, and people will appreciate the extra money."

Earl looked at me, skepticism still in his eyes.

"Let me think about it. I'll let you know tomorrow."

With that I gathered my things and went to my office. I sat at my desk and thought about why it was that I was so different. It seemed that I was always going against management, when all I was doing was trying to do what was right; what was best for the individual and what was best for the company. True, I could have not said anything to Earl about a hiring freeze. No one would have faulted me for that. After all, no one else was talking about hiring freeze. But I saw the numbers, and I couldn't, without a guilty conscious, at least make an attempt to express what I believed we needed to do. The next day I saw Earl in the hallway. He stopped me and said,

"Go ahead and draft a memo for me about freezing all hiring, except for critical positions. Have it ready for me to send out today."

"Thank you, Earl" I replied.

Now I know how Noah felt. But he had 99 years, I only had one year and a couple of months. For the next 12 months, other organizations continued to hire, and the numbers were growing. During this time, when I met with my Financial Management team they would ask if we still had a freeze on hiring. When I responded that we did, they would look at each other, shrug their shoulders and pretend like they didn't ask the question. It was like, "He doesn't get it, does he." It finally happened at about the 14th month mark. When I joined the company, we had 15,000 employees. It peaked at 16,000. Manufacturing's first layoff was about five percent of its work force or about 400 people. It was just the beginning. Because of our freeze on hiring, Quality didn't have a layoff until two years into the depression. Strange, during those two years, no one came to me to ask, "How did you know" or say, "Good move." But the prior two years, skepticism was dripping. Projections had us growing the Quality organization from 900 to 1200 people during the two years we had the freeze. Since we didn't hire the people, eliminating all the benefits and excess staffing, the savings to the company was huge. But again, there was neither recognition nor reward. The consolation I had was that I knew I had saved the lives of many families.

"Civilians don't often appreciate nor reward leadership, innovation, or dedication. The service does and has recognized innate leadership in you; which, will not necessarily be so in the civilian sector where politics and envy can come into play." Gen. Olds.

One late afternoon, as Earl's staff was in his office waiting for him to arrive, a topic of department morale came up.

"You know the lay-offs are really hurting morale; and Earl keeps pushing folks to work harder and to an increasingly higher standard. Some of the folks think he has no pity." One of the Directors said.

"Yeah. He's been pushing us, and we have been pushing our folks." Another said.

"Do you think we can get him to slack up just a little?" Another asked.

The conversation went on in this vein for about ten minutes, until Earl entered the room.

"Hi guys, what do you think should be our number one topic today?" Earl asked as he looked around the room. All eight guys began mumbling about different things but none made mention of the topic that they had just spent 10 minutes talking about.

"Well Earl, we just finished having a discussion about department morale and that almost all of the Quality organization is being impacted. If we don't address it, it could have an impact on the next Government audit scheduled in two months," I said.

"OK, I heard rumors of a morale issue, but nothing concrete, what do you guys say. Do we have a morale problem or not?" Earl asked.

"No, I don't think we do. Folks are working hard and are concerned about the layoffs in the other departments, wondering when they are going to be impacted. In contrast to the other departments, I think morale is pretty good in the Quality organization." One of the Directors said.

"OK. What about the rest of you guys? Do you feel the same way?"

"Yeah, I think morale, for us anyway, is pretty good."

"Well Mel, what were you talking about, morale being fairly low? The guys evidently don't think so." Earl said.

"Earl, we just spent 10 minutes or so on this topic just before you came in; however, if the guys think morale has improved from that time until now, then I have nothing to say."

It was amazing to me the lack of backbone the guys had. Sure, Earl is tough, but one thing I told Earl when I accepted the position, I will always be straight with him. All I asked in return was that he not penalize me for being the bearer of bad news. These guys are older than I am, had been in Quality much, much longer, and had Earls respect. Yet, since most of the morale issue was being placed on Earl, none wanted to bring it up; and, possibly be the fall guy. However, they were very willing to hang me out to dry, since, as a result of their denial, my comment didn't seem to have substance. I had a momentary thought of 'how do I get even?' but quickly suppressed it. I thought, since I manage the finances of the whole organization, I could really get even. Sometimes it would be nice to put the Christian cloak down for just a moment. Fortunately, or unfortunately, I was concerned that if I laid it down, it would not be there when I went to pick it up again. So, I suppressed the thought.

Renee's 40th

About two months before Renee turned 40, we had some friends over and the subject of age came up. We were all talking, and out of the blue, Renee said,

"I'm going to have a big party for my fortieth, even if I have to give it myself."

Little was Renee aware that things had already been set in motion for her birthday.

The Friday before her birthday, we went to "Covenant Couples," a group meeting at Orlando Christian Center where about 30 – 40 couples would meet. The group would meet twice a month. We were leaders in the group and Pastors Sam and Steve facilitated the sessions. We would study the Word, have small group sessions, and occasionally have an

International Cook Out. This particular Friday was an International Cook Out were each couple brought something from their country or state of origin. As a result of this, there was a lot of intermingling and conversation. However, not one person said to Renee, "Happy Birthday." On the way home, Renee was not a happy camper. After all, we were leaders in the group, surely someone should have remembered her birthday. In exasperation, Renee repeated what she had said two months earlier, "I will have a big birthday party even if I have to give it to myself." I kept my eyes on the road and said nothing.

The following day, Saturday, I had to coach one of Dez's soccer games. Usually Renee would go with us, but on this particular day she was so despondent she chose not to. After all, it was her birthday and no one seemed to care; and besides, it wasn't just any ol' birthday, it was number 40. As I was leaving out the door for the game, I told Renee that a couple of friends were coming over, that we were going out for an early dinner, and that she had to be ready by 3:00 PM. As fate would have it, the game prior went into overtime, and Dez's game did as well. We won the game, but the overtimes put me about 30 minutes behind schedule. Now you have to understand, Renee is never, ever, ready on-time for anything. I came rushing into the house to take a shower and change clothes.

Renee looks at me and says in a very sarcastic manner, "At least I'm ready."

Yeah, right, the one time I'm running late, she's ready. I go in to shower, change clothes, and go downstairs where Renee is "patiently" waiting. I look at my watch, not time yet. I need a few more minutes. At that moment, our neighbor, Bob, knocks on the backdoor. Yes! Whatever he wants I will milk it for an extra five minutes.

"Mel, do you have a channel lock and a 9/16" wrench?"

"Sure Bob. I'll get it for you. What are you working on? Do you need some help?"

As I walk out the back door, I dare not look at Renee. Bob's issue was a quick fix. So, as I come back into the house, the baby-sitter, Andrita, arrives. While I'm going over some things with Andrita, the door-bell rings. Al 'right, now we're cooking. Renee goes to answer the door. She is greeted by a stranger who proceeds to ask for her and myself. With a flourish, he bows, extends his hand, and steps aside so that she can see out the door and unto the driveway. There sitting in the driveway is a black limousine. I get our movie camera which I had hidden by the door earlier. Renee goes out the door and cautiously approaches the limo. The way she was walking you would have thought it was a kid-napping or a hearse. She opens the door and is greeted by... my sister, her dad, Phil and Kathy and the Morrisons.

My sister, Vic, who came in from Los Angeles, was by the door and Renee kept hitting her.

"What (hit) are you (hit) doing here (hit, hit)?

I had flown my sister and Renee's dad in from Los Angeles and had them stay with Phil and Kathy the night before. Renee had no idea that they were even in town. We got in the Limo and drove to a restaurant on the east side of Orlando, about a 40-minute ride. During the course of the meal, we were laughing and giggling so much the waiter stop and said,

"Now I know I have only brought water for you guys to drink, did you sneak in something of your own? If you did, I think I would like to try a little."

"Naah, we just brought Phil along," I said.

Dinner was a great time. It was dusk by the time we were getting back into the limo, and just before I ducked my head into the limo, I looked at the sun, it was a gorgeous sunset. It reminded me of another sunset so long ago when I was back in college. Oh well, God is good. Incidentally, we paid for the Limo driver's dinner as well. What a difference in his performance. He was nice before, but he doubled up on the niceness.

We continued with the laughter and fun. It is hard not to laugh when Phil is around. He is like a grown-up kid. He has no shame. He has a talent to mimic people's voices and their expressions and often times I am his favorite subject. As he imitated my voice and mannerism, I couldn't help but to laugh along with everyone else. Before we left the restaurant, I very discretely excused myself. I found a phone and placed a call (cell phones were not fully introduced yet). The ride back to our home went very fast. Our home is one of three homes at the very end of a short Cul-de-sac. The street on which we lived was about a quarter of a mile from the street that ran into the main entrance. So, as we turned off the main street and onto a branch that led to our home, Renee started to notice an unusual number of cars along the road. All of us tried to keep her distracted, but she wouldn't buy it. Just as the limo made the left turn into the Cul-de-sac, the driver stopped the car and opened the sun roof. Renee stood up, head sticking out of the limo and took in the scene. People had lined up along each side of our driveway and out into each side of Cul-de-sac. Renee began the "Queens wave" as the limo driver inched his way forward. Our friends had made signs, "Lordy, Lordy, look who's forty." "The Way we Were must be your favorite song." It was great. Renee was enjoying it all.

We got out of the limo and went into the house. There must have been about 150 people in total. Many of the folks from Covenant Couple were there. A friend ran up to Renee and said,

"Renee, I so badly wanted to say Happy Birthday to you last night, but I was afraid that I would say something to give tonight away. In fact, that is why no one said anything to you."

Tears welled up in Renee's eyes as she realized that it was because of the love that people had for her that kept them from saying Happy Birthday, not that they didn't care. No one wanted to be the one to ruin the surprise that was planned for her. Meanwhile, we had another half hour on the limo. What to do? The limo driver noticed the number of teens and kids and offered to make two trips of 15 minutes each, giving them an opportunity to take a limo ride. Talk about excitement. We split them into two groups and off they went. When the limo driver finished his time and I went out to pay him, he said,

"There are not a lot of times when I get to enjoy the people I am with, but you guys have made this a fun day. Thank you."

His comment was very appreciative as I thanked God that he saw a difference in us. Meanwhile, back in the house, the party was in full swing. We opened the double doors between the living and family room and the triple sliding door from the family room to the patio area was open, so there was a lot of space for all the people in attendance. What was great to see was the mix of races and nationality. When Renee and I are invited to a party, many times, if it were our White friends, we would be the only Black couple. When we went to a party with our Black friends, there would be no one there that was White. However, whenever we had something happening at our home, we always had a mix of races. This was no exception. The neat thing about it was that there was no grouping or clicks. Blacks with Blacks or Whites with just Whites. It was a true intermingling. We had a few talented friends that could really sing, so we had a mini concert, then later, one of the members of the church band got on our piano and began playing. From that moment on it turned into a hallelujah night. It was after midnight before people started going home and after 1:00 AM before the stragglers began to leave.

Renee had her "Big" birthday party, even though she didn't have to give it to herself.

Renee's New Car

Buying a new car for most people is quite stressful and very unpleasant. Me, I don't mind the haggling; however, I don't like unscrupulous behavior. Shortly after Renee's birthday, I decided to buy her a new car. Shopping around, I thought a Toyota Camry would be a good car to replace the Dodge Colt Vista since we had gotten a conversion van as a third vehicle. With a sedan, Renee wouldn't look like a "Soccer Mom" everywhere she went. So unbeknownst to Renee I did some shopping around. (Once again this was before the internet, so much of the shopping was done by driving around.) I drive to a couple of Toyota dealers near me with little success. Getting a little frustrated at having no success, I gather Renee and told her we are going for a drive. I wanted to surprise her, but I also wanted her to be a part of getting the car, after all, it was going to be hers. At one dealership when Renee was not with me, the manager said that he would sell the car at my asking price.

"Mr. King, I will sell you the car you want, but only if you buy the car right now."

"I can't do that. I need to have my wife look at the car."

"You are paying for the car, aren't you?

"Yes, I am."

"Well, I buy a car for my wife, I just by it. I'm the one who is paying for it."

"I may be the one paying for it, but it will be hers and she has a right to decide. Thank you for your time." With that I excused myself and walked out.

I locate another dealership; this one is on the northeast side of Orlando. Renee and I go on the lot and wait for a salesman.

"Hi, my wife and I are interested in a Toyota Camry, red with gold insignia. You got anything on the lot like that?"

"Don't think so. However, we won't let that stop us from making a deal. We'll trade with another dealer if we have to." The salesman said.

"Let's sit down and see what kind of pricing you have and let's see if we can make a deal. By the way, I want you to know that you are the third dealership that I am speaking to. Just want you to know I'm serious about buying if you are serious about selling.'

"Oh, I'm sure we can make a deal."

We walk into his office, exchange names and begin discussions.

"Now, tell me what you want on the car. Once I have all the features you want, I can work up a price."

"Before we go there, are there any promotions going on? If so, obviously I would like to take advantage of them."

"Yes, one excellent promotion we have is our leasing program. With $2500 down, you can drive out of here today in a brand-new Camry."

I asked a few more questions about the program and then did a few calculations.

"OK, let's discuss the leasing program later. Right now, I think I want to by the car. Here's a list of what I'm looking for and I am willing to pay $18,000."

The salesman did a few calculations himself.

"I'm sorry the best I can do is $19,500. However, I can get you into our leasing program for just $1500 down."

"OK, but no thanks. Thanks for your time."

"Wait a minute Mr. King, let me go and get my manager. Maybe he can make a deal."

"OK. Don't mind waiting a couple of minutes. The number is firm though."

"Hi Mr. King, I'm Fred. Let's see if we can get you into a new Camry."

"I'm hoping that you can."

After about another half hour, they agreed on the $18,000.

"You know we don't have the car on the lot so I will have to make a dealer trade to get it here. Give us a week, and we'll call you when it is ready for pick-up."

We conclude the deal and Renee is pleased with her new car. As it turns out, Renee's Dad, Al, is out visiting the week that I get a call, on a Tuesday, from the dealership.

Mr. King this is the Toyota dealer, we're calling to let you know that the Camry is here and is ready for pick-up."

"That is great. However, I won't be able to pick it up until this Saturday. Is that OK?"

"That is fine. I'll let the manager know."

Saturday morning Al and I drive out to the dealership to pick up the Camry.

"Hi John, I'm back to pick up the Camry."

"OK, let's go in the office."

"Mel, you know we have this great leasing program that will only cost you $1500 to get you into a brand-new Camry."

"John, we went through this. Yes $1500, to get in but $24,000 over the life of the program when I factor in mileage. I told you I am not interested. I am here to pick up my car."

"The car is not here. We can't do the deal at the $18,000. You see, as a dealer trade, there are some extra costs that factor in that prevents us from doing the deal at that price."

"You guys called me Tuesday and said that the car was here on the lot. Is it here, yes, or no?"

"No, the car is not here."

"Then you lied. You said the car was here. Why do you think I have my father-in-law with me? To drive my car back home. Ok, I'm outta here. I will call Toyota Corporate on this."

When I called Toyota Corporate, and told them my story, they offered no reconciliation or any incentive to purchase a

Camry given that I was lied to. I crossed Camry off our list of vehicles. In fact, I crossed Toyota off our list of car companies from which we would ever purchase a vehicle.

After a couple of days, I stopped at a Mazda dealership. Mazda just came out with a new design for their 626 and, to me, was equal to the Camry but much better looking than the old 626 model. Renee also liked the body style just as well as the Camry. The dealership and I haggled back and forth a little bit, but we made a deal and we bought a red Mazda 626, hassle-free. As I said, I don't mind the negotiating, but only when it is done in good faith.

A Sad Day

A friend of ours, Doug a financial planner, stopped by one day and asked me about my finances and if they were in order. We went through a review and helped me in some areas that needed attention. I was so impressed by what he did that I introduced him to Bob and Carol, our neighbor. Carol was a mom and housewife. The two youngest of three children were still at home. It was very fortunate that this meeting transpired. Doug helped Bob set up accounts that he, Bob, funded and could take advantage of various financial vehicles offered by his company. Three months later, Bob was playing basketball and had a heart attack. He died shortly thereafter. As a result of the financial strategy that Doug was able to set up, for Bob and Carol, Carol was able to keep the house, in addition to providing an income for Carol and the two youngest daughters.

Quality Newsletter and Politics

Along with financial management, people management, Cost of Quality management, Audits, Policy & Procedures, Special Projects management, etc. I was asked to take on the task of re-starting a Quality Newsletter. This assignment happened sometime near the end of my tenure as the Quality Business Manager, and before I became a Quality Project Manager. The organization had been without a newsletter for a number of years; and, the Quality management team believed that there was a lot of information and important current events that needed to get disseminated to the entire Quality organization. I became the senior editor as I pulled individuals in to assist me from throughout the Quality organization. We were able to get our first edition published in about two months with excellent reviews. The Newsletter would be issued quarterly for the first two issues, then monthly thereafter. As the months went by, we improved the Newsletter to the point where it became the de facto standard for any other organization newsletter.

The irony, my replacement, as I was being moved to be the Quality Manager on the Brilliant Pebbles program, received recognition by the quality management team for publishing the newsletter.

I thought, "The injustice of it all." By the time my replacement came on board, most of the creative, development, and logistics planning had been done and was in place. All this other manager had to do was to keep doing what I and my team had done prior to his replacing me. This obvious ignoring of my contribution seemed to be the norm with Martin Marietta. A lack of recognition for my performance seems to hold especially true for the Finance Department (A Glass unbroken). I was disappointed that the Quality organization had now done something similar. Of all the millions of dollars that I have saved the company, the exceptional recognition that I brought to the company through the various programs that I managed; and coaching a ragtag group of folks into a viable and a very productive organization, I never received acknowledgement from my financial management team. In fact, at my yearly assessment, I spoke with the Finance Director, in which I reported, about my accomplishments.

"Frank, since I have been at Martin Marietta, and all the things that I have done for the company, such as: Total Quality Management, the Contractor Performance Certification Program, Reduction of a projected $14 million over-run to a $200 thousand underrun in one year, to the untold millions that I have saved and continue to save by putting a freeze on hiring, I never received recognition nor a bonus for my efforts. There are guys who haven't done a quarter of the things that I have done, but have received both, bonuses and recognition. Personally, I would rather receive the bonus." I said to start off the meeting.

"Mel, what you say is true. In fact, the things that you have accomplished are very verifiable, whereas, many times management does give out bonuses where you may have to stretch the imagination. It is good that we are having this conversation."

"Frank, I understand that I am not with the 'In-crowd;' however, it is extremely unfair to totally ignore my contributions. Finance hasn't even seen fit to rate me a level one employee. I would challenge Finance to compare my accomplishments to any person who they have rated a level one. I am not satisfied at being a level two employee; and I believe my performance would substantiate my assertions."

"Mel, I am not going to make promises, but I do agree with you. You are deserving of a level one, and I will see what I can do."

After about two months of effort, Frank called me into his office to tell me that he was unsuccessful in his attempt to get a bonus, recognition or a level one rating for me. He apologized and reiterated that he seriously tried.

"Civilians don't often appreciate nor reward leadership, innovation, or dedication. The service does and has recognized innate leadership in you; which, will not necessarily be so in the civilian sector where politics and envy can come into play." General Olds.

Martin Marietta Missile Systems
PRODUCT ASSURANCE PROFILES

Vol. 4, No. 3   March 1990

DIRECTOR'S BYLINE
By: Ron F. Swiger

CHANGING OF THE GUARD

I want to take this opportunity to express my appreciation and say thank you to all of you, the Product Assurance employees and to my staff, for your support and encouragement during my first few weeks as Missile System's Product Assurance Director. We have many challenges ahead of us; however, I want to encourage you to continue the outstanding job that the Government and industry have come to recognize as a company trademark.

During the leadership of Earl Mills, there has been significant progress in the quality of our service, hardware, and customer relations here at Missile Systems. This progress must continue, and, at the risk of sounding trite, we know it is you, the employees, that will make it happen.

I have had the opportunity to meet with my staff individually. Shortly I will begin to "walk the floor" to meet many of you and to reacquaint myself with those of you I have worked with over the years. I believe we have a great team that has provided demonstrated excellence, and, as a team, I have every confidence that we will build on the process of continuous improvement.

On behalf of myself and my staff I want to once again thank you for your continued support and encouragement. In certain issues, this column will be devoted to answering questions of interest to you. We will try to respond to the most frequently asked questions that are appropriate for this forum. To submit a question, send it to Bill Hennessy, MP 301.

Sitting, L-R: Kermit Gay, Mel King, Ron Swiger, Dick Adkins; Standing, L-R: Robert Miller, Bill Coral, Paul Nolin, Leon Newton, Sam Maloof, Bill Hennessy, Dave West, Jim Hooper, James Carrol, Robert Mellor, Ed Samuels, Brad Johnson.

SHOP TALK
By: R. Nichol

Finally, after 9 months of being almost constantly subjected to audits and shop tours, Missile Systems and all of its employees have been honored for their hard work. Becoming (CP)² certified is a most coveted reward that places us among the elite of defense contractors. It is also a beacon that says to our customers, our employees, and our communities that we are committed to being a quality organization. Now is a good time to think about how far we have come, what we have gained, and where we are heading.

The past few years have seen many changes. Among these was a true effort to become a superior company. For most of us, reflecting on the first POS audit brings back nightmares. However, from that time until now, we have built a solid foundation and have rapidly made adjustments that are leading to a process of continuous improvements. By constantly raising our standards, overcoming obstacles, and surpassing established goals, we have set new standards in our jobs. The effects of succeeding and becoming one of the best in the business go beyond the confines of perimeter road. The pride that we have in our performance and our commitment to quality and excellence reaches all aspects of our lives. Our families, our communities, and our country all reap the benefits of our successes.

For all of us, (CP)² is not the climax of our efforts, but rather it is the base that we shall build on. We must continue to constantly improve. We must use our experience, and tools such as the PMTs and SPC, to set even higher standards. Perfection is something rarely reached, but it is one goal worth striving for.

As you look at the photo, L-R, I am sitting second and then Ron Swiger, Quality Director

PRODUCT ASSURANCE PROFILES PAGE 4

FAADS U.S. Army Release

Soldiers using the Army's proposed Line of Sight-Forward-Heavy (LOS-F-H) battlefield air defense system shot down six of seven aircraft in the live missile firing portion of the weapon's initial operational test and evaluation.

The tests at White Sands Missile Range, New Mexico, from February 13 to February 20 were against fixed-wing jet fighters and helicopters using tactics and countermeasures representative of Soviet attack aircraft. The tests were conducted under conditions as close to realistic battlefield conditions as possible. Firings were conducted during day and night and against a variety of electronic and infrared countermeasures using various attack profiles at varying ranges.

The Army's Operational Test and Evaluation Agency (OTEA) conducted the tests and will evaluate data to determine how well the LOS-F-H provides low-altitude air defense protection for tanks and personnel carriers on the battlefield. That includes an assessment of weapon performance as well as the doctrine, tactics, and procedures developed for its use.

The soldiers who conducted the firings are from the 2nd Battalion, 6th Air Defense Brigade, based at Ft. Bliss, Texas.

A LOS-F-H fire unit carries eight ready-to-fire guided missiles, a radar, two lasers to determine distance to the target and to guide the missile in flight, and passive infrared and TV sensors for target tracking and engagement, all mounted on a single tracked vehicle. The fire unit is operated by a crew of three enlisted soldiers: gunner, radar operator, and driver.

LOS-F-H operational testing will resume in April at Ft. Hunter-Liggett, California, where the weapon's performance in simulated combat between two armored forces will be evaluated. No missiles will be fired in that phase of the test.

FROM THE EDITOR By: M. King

This will be the last issue of *Profiles* of which I am editor. I want to thank Presentations, those who have submitted articles, those who promised they would submit articles, the customer, and others who have contributed to the success of *Profiles*. Thanks are also given to Sam Maloof and John McBrite, who at various times were assistant editors; and a special thanks to Leslie Thomas, who stuck through all the deadlines, panics, and promises.

I pass the editorial pen over to Mr. William (Bill) Hennessy and extend my well wishes. Future issues of *Profiles* will be published bimonthly.

Martin Marietta Missile Systems
P.O. Box 555837
Orlando, Florida 32855-5837

MARTIN MARIETTA
© Martin Marietta Corporation 1990

PRODUCT ASSURANCE PROFILES
S T A F F
Mel King: Editor   Leslie Thomas: Associate Editor
                           Paul Elliott: Associate Editor
                           (Ocala)

Submit your articles to: Mel King – MP 301, Ext 02251

I can only thank the Lord that I was often reminded by Holy Spirit that I don't work for man, but for Him. So many times, I had performed above and beyond senior management's expectation and neither received the recognition nor reward for my performance. Occasionally, several Directors or Vice Presidents would make comment to me, unofficially, but their comments never got put into action, such as a bonus or promotion. I have to say, that my knowing that I work for the Lord kept me from becoming bitter. Lord knows I had reason to.

Another irony, when I left my position as the Quality Business Manager, it took three other managers to do what I was doing. One manager to do the financials, another to do Policy and Procedures, and another for Cost of quality and the various special projects.

Community Recognition

What can I say? Companies seem to have a hard time recognizing my accomplishments, but other entities don't seem to have that problem. The following article was published in an Orlando local newspaper, circa 1991. As you read the article, the awards mentioned were not from the company, but from entities that I supported that was as a result of my Quality position with Lockheed Martin.

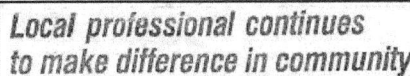

Local professional continues to make difference in community

By Michele Austin
Editorial Assistant

When a leader is needed to assist in training counselors and providing counsel to church members, he counsels. When school policies and procedures need to be established, he supports. And, when the Association of Christian Youth Sports needs a soccer coach, he volunteers.

The well-rounded, energetic individual is Mel S.C. King, Quality Program Manager for Martin Marietta Orlando Aerospace.

As Quality Program Manager, he is responsible for the management of labor, policy application and budget for Product Assurance on-site, field and off-site functions for the mission area. He also establishes quality program plans, conducts contractor compliance surveys and technical capability evaluations.

A native of Indianapolis, Indiana, King received a Bachelor of Science in Finance from California State in 1975 and acquired his MBA from Loyola Marymount in 1979.

When asked what experiences in life contributed to his successful outcome, he says that there were two things. First, he expressed his sense of independence which evolved at a young age. "Being the sixth of eight children, there was not a lot of time afforded me by my parents," he said. "Consequently, self-motivation was a requirement for any success and continues with me today," he added.

The second influence which occurred later in life, was his developing a strong belief in God. "The many challenges in this world are easier to face and overcome when you know there is someone other than yourself working to gain the victory," he replied.

See KING page 10

King

Speaking Engagement at Central Florida University

KING
Continued from page 1

Because of his hard work and dedication, King has received several awards, honors and recognitions for his achievements. He was recently elected, Vice-Chairman and Publicity Chairman of the Orlando chapter of the American Society for Quality Control, he received the President's Award from the Martin Management Club in recognition for leading the company into Total Quality Management and was awarded the Henry DeZwart Award from the American Society for Quality Control for his outstanding contribution.

Although he plans to continue to strive to be the best quality manager within the company, the highly versatile businessman has an interest in politics that he has plans to explore in the future.

During my time as Quality Program Manager, I was asked to speak about Quality to a group of Engineering students at the University of Central Florida. I thought for a couple of days and asked myself, "How can I make this interesting and something that they won't forget? Engineers habitually don't like Quality types." An idea came to mind that resulted in me going to a toy store to pick up four water guns and a toy airplane. These were going to be my props for an object lesson, so when I got home, I dismantled the firing mechanism in one of the water guns.

On the day of my scheduled speaking, I walk into the lecture hall. I had spoken with the professor earlier that day and a couple days prior, so he had material about my background to establish me as someone that knew quality.

Immediately, I spoke about the continuing "Hatfield & McCoy" war that exist between Engineering and Quality.

I said, "I want you to know that every person that works in Quality knows that Engineering doesn't like them. Today, you may wonder why that is, however, once you get out in the real world of Engineering, it won't take long before your peers will begin brainwashing you. They will tell you all the horror stories of why YOU should not be friends with Quality; and, 'all that Quality does is put road blocks in front of your designs to keep them from being built.'

That is partially true. Quality is a road block, and thankfully so, for poor engineering and designs. Let me give you an example. May I have four volunteers?"

Of course, I didn't say what I needed volunteers for, so there was not a rush to respond to my question.

"OK, so you know that I work for a defense contractor. So, let me show you how important a good design, and good Quality Control, work together, for a good defense. The reason why I needed four volunteers is that I brought four water guns. . . "

Before I finished, multiple hands went up, all guys. I selected four and made two teams, two people per team.

"Now we, no you guys are going to have a five second water fight. I spaced the teams about 10 feet apart. Begin when I say 'Go' and, please stop when I say 'Stop.'"

"OK, 'Go'" I said.

Immediately one of the four complained that his water gun was not working.

"Hey. My gun is not working. Hey, guys that's not fair."

As is typical of human nature, the two guys on the opposing team began to take advantage of the weakness of the other team. As soon as they heard his gun was not working, both of the other team members focused their water guns on him. I let this go on beyond the five seconds, maybe a total of seven seconds or so.

"All right, 'Stop,'" I said.

I asked the one student, "How did you feel, once you found out your weapon did not work?"

"I felt cheated, left out, hopeless, and the fact that both of them started shooting at me I thought was unfair." The student said.

"However, that is what the enemy does, once a weakness is discovered, every attempt is made to exploit it.

"You guys were using water, what if they were real guns with real bullets? How would you have felt then? The purpose of Quality is to make sure that your designs work and work the way you designed them. Obviously, one of the water guns did not work the way it was designed, with a little help of course, however, you can see how your fellow classmate felt when what he thought was a perfectly good water gun didn't function. For as short a period of time as it was, the other three had fun, he did not. They all three got wet, perhaps he more than the others. And, I suspect his disappointment was primarily due because he couldn't participate and fight back." I said to the class.

"Now, let's get a couple of more volunteers." There was a slight reluctance but I was able to get two more candidates.

I took out the toy airplane, put two conference tables together and told one of the students to stand about 30 feet away.

"The object of this lesson is to land that plane on this runway. These two tables are the runway, just in case you didn't know."

"Oh, well, that's easy." Said the student.

"Blindfolded," I said.

I looked at the other student. "I just happened to have a blindfold, please put this on him. And make sure he can't peek around the side or anything."

The one student went to put the blindfold on the one holding the plane.

"OK, good. Now I would make this extremely difficult by turning you around a couple of times but we won't do that, this time. OK, put the plane out in front of you and land on the runway. By the way, you have to walk at a normal pace. No stopping, slowing down, or moving sideways. You are a pilot of a passenger jet with 150 souls on board. Begin your landing. By the way, no help from the class please."

As the student began to walk, immediately there were, "Ooh Oh," "Can't look," "Hope they took out flight insurance," "Crash and burn."

I looked at the professor, he was grinning from ear to ear. The class was engaged and he was enjoying it. Obviously, the student didn't come anywhere close to landing on the tables.

"One of the aspects about Quality is to try to have whatever is designed, operate correctly, 100% of the time. How secure would you feel if the airlines said that you have an 85% chance of arriving safely at your destination? No takers with those odds. How about 99%? Still no takers. How about 100%? I thought so, the whole class. Well, that is what Quality is all about. Landings equaling take-offs."

I could see the light go on with many of the students as they began nodding their heads in understanding and hopefully, agreement.

"Alright, let's try landing again, but this time let's make a few changes. This time, I want you to talk the student in to the runway. You'll see there will be some lessons learned in this scenario as well."

We positioned the student, we'll call him John, 30 feet away again and the person talking we'll call Bill. I forgot to mention that the planes altitude started with the student's arm raised as high as he can reach.

"OK, begin"

"All right John move to your left, your other left. Not that much. Back to the right. Begin lowering the plane. Lower, lower, hold. You're drifting to the right come back left.

By now, John, who is maintaining a normal walk has closed the distance much faster than what Bill thought and now Bill's instructions are becoming more frantic and louder. Meanwhile the class is starting to break into tears with their laughter. Bill was so focused on landing the plane that he forgot that he had to steer John just to the left of the table so that the "plane" can land on the runway. Before he realized his mistake, it was too late to recover. It was a crashed landing.

"Ok Class, what did you see that went wrong that could have helped to prevent the crash?"

"Come to an agreement on how much to move, when moving left or right?" a student said.

"Also, how much to move up or down," another student said.

"Determine how far to lower his arm when told to do so?" Another student said.

"OK. Very Good. Let's put those practices in place," I said.

This time Bill, using established procedures, guided John, in for a successful landing and the class erupted. The professor's grin got even wider.

"What I hope you leaned out of this object lesson were several key things, 1) Establish policies and procedures, first; 2) Have a 'Lessons Learned' session after a failure or success; 3) Document your procedure; 4) Make sure everyone who is responsible understands and has agreed to follow the process; and, 5) Make sure you operate within design specifications. Thank you for having me in you class today."

From there I went into some of the aspects of Quality and provided examples and illustrations of real events.

A couple days later the Quality Director called me into his office.

"Mel, I got a letter from a professor at the University of Central Florida. He says that he wanted to thank Martin Marietta for letting you come to his class and speak on the subject of Quality. He says he has never seen his class so engaged and a subject so well demonstrated. It goes on to say that he believes a lasting impression, the right impression, of Quality has been made on his Engineering students as a result of your presentation.

Mel, this is just another example of your continued good representation of the Quality organization. We are really fortunate to have you on the team. Good job." Earl, the Quality Director said.

Trips to Los Angeles

As Aaron and Dez got older and were able to travel alone on an airplane, we would send them to Los Angeles during the summer months to spend about four weeks with their grandparents, Al and Amay. While in L.A. their

grandparents would take them to many of the local tourist areas such as Disneyland, the beach, Long Beach Harbor, Knotts Berry Farm, San Diego Zoo, Marine Land, and many other places.

Every other Christmas we, as a family, would fly to L.A., and while there, it was a custom to go skiing on Desiree's birthday, 23rd of December. We would go to either Mountain High or Snow Valley, each of which were about one hour and 45 minutes away. On one occasion, their grandmother (60), and aunt (48) went with us. It was their first-time skiing. In the photo is: Renee, Myrna (Renee's sister, Sandra (Aunt), Mel, Amay, in front - Desiree and Aaron.

Becoming a Quality Program Manager
Brilliant Pebbles

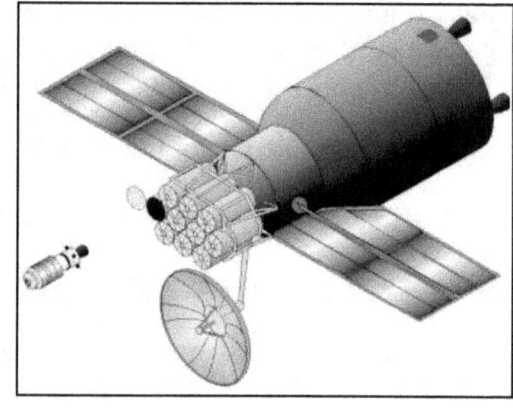

It became very apparent to the Quality organization that Finance did not appreciate my talents; so much so that the Quality Director asked to have me transferred into his organization. The Quality Director was well aware of the sacrifice I made in order to support his division. His comment to me was,

"Mel, we get you into our organization we can take care of you. It's obvious that Finance has not and will not."

I agreed to the transfer and became the Quality Program Manager of the Brilliant Pebble (BP) program, a subset of the "Star Wars" project initiated by President Ronald Reagan. It was called Brilliant Pebbles because of the size and intelligence of the kill vehicle. Most satellite kill vehicles were controlled from the ground, from launch to termination. This unit had its own intelligence and did not need to be in contact with the ground for terminal guidance. It is a space based defensive weapon. Once the command was given to launch, the small missile would guide itself to the target, hitting it and kill it with kinetic energy. There was no warhead. We had one success after another on the program. Then President Clinton came into office. He was not fond of the Star Wars program and used the money allocated to the project to fund his Bosnia campaign. Every time I read in the newspaper that $30 million was being spent in Bosnia, I knew my program would get hit by the same amount. It was not long thereafter that we were asked to shut the program down.

At one point in the testing cycle a test unit, myself, and about eight other engineers were at the Redstone Arsenal, in Alabama, conducting outer space testing. The bay was totally black, which created a huge walking hazard. It was very difficult to delineate lines or separation of objects so we always had to walk holding on to something. It was not unusual, while working or conducting a test, to hear coming out of the darkness, "Ouch," "What the heck," and other expletives. As the days went by, our navigation of the bay improved significantly. When it came time to send the unit back to Orlando for final fit-out, I had the responsibility of sealing the truck in which the vehicle was being carried. There was a combination lock, of which only I knew the combo, three witnesses, paper tape to seal the back, and my signature on the release document. This was heady stuff. As it was, no one, other than myself, was to have access to the unit until I released it when it arrives back in Orlando. The drive down was to take 24 hours. The team and I flew back to Orlando to wait on the unit's arrival.

On the day of arrival, there was a little gathering as a small group of people waited at the back gate for the arrival of the truck and its precious cargo. We had a few senior management team members present and of course, they all wanted to have first peek at the unit. It had been kept in a cloud of secrecy while at the facility prior to being shipped to Redstone, so I guess they figured they would have a chance to see it now. As the truck entered the gate and pulled to a waiting parking lot, the group, en-masse, surged to the truck. I was a little behind and walked casually to the truck. The driver got out, clip board in hand, and said "Is there a Mel King here?" From the back of the group,

"That would be me" I answered.

It was like the parting of the Red Sea, albeit small, but still a parting. I checked the seals, the lock and the paperwork. Additionally, I had noted a small nick on the truck prior to leaving Redstone, just for me to have assurance that it was the same cargo trailer. I accepted the delivery and had a fork-lift standing by. We opened the back and the crate was still anchored and in position. The group of managers that gathered to see the unit were disappointed but reminded themselves that this was a high security clearance project, a clearance of which none of them had. This was going to be about as close as they were going to get to the unit. We took the unit and put it in a secured, ultra clean room, with a shroud around the unit itself. It remained here until it was shipped to Edwards AFB, California for testing. The test was extremely successful.

A New Brilliant Pebbles

Shortly after the testing of the original unit, Martin Marietta and Lockheed would become one company - Lockheed Martin. It was during the time of the merger process we were asked to build a second unit. I and my Quality team (about six individuals) were the only ones that were carried over. The fact that we were part of the team proved instrumental in its success. On the initial briefing the program manager was talking to all of the personnel that would work on the project. He outlined some of the major functions of the unit, how it was going to go together and when he expected the project to be completed. As he was talking, I began taking some notes. He finished and asked the Technical Director (TD) make a few comments. Then the inevitable rhetorical question "Are there any questions?" I raised my hand. The TD was surprised but acknowledged me. He and I had not met before so I introduced Myself;

"My name is Mel King; I am the Quality Manager on the program. I do have a few comments I would like to make."

From my perspective, I was stunned that there was not one engineer from the previous build. If there was, then I would not have had to say what I did.

"Sir, at this point this project would be subject to failure and an extreme over-run." All side conversations stopped and it got really quiet.

"Sir, as much as Engineering and Quality fight, my job is to help make this project successful. You mentioned about replenishing the fuel supply and conducting multiple live testing of the unit. It can't be done. The fuel tanks on the unit are 'Once and Done' tanks. There is no port for refilling."

There were a couple of other things that I had mentioned that the engineering team was unawares. When I stopped talking, all eyes shifted from me and looked at either the Program Manager or the TD for direction. The two of them were looking at each other.

"Well, it looks like we had better have a meeting with Quality before we go off and do something stupid."

There was a little chuckle from the audience. The Program Director and TD met with me and my team and I gave a de-briefing on the problems and Lessons Learned from the previous unit, something that should have been done at the first. As have happened in the past, and seems to be a continuing pattern with Martin Marietta, now Lockheed Martin, there was neither recognition of the contribution nor reward for the averted disaster that would have occurred had the program proceeded on its initial course.

A few months after the meeting to discuss the second build, a joint program meeting, with Lockheed Martin and the Air Force, was to occur in at the Lockheed facility near Denver. I was walking in a hallway going to my office when the program manager stopped me.

"Hey, Mel. You got a minute?" He asked.

"Sure Jackson, what's up?" I said.

"Do you know about the project meeting that's in Denver next week?"

"Yes, I do."

"Are you going?"

"No, I hadn't planned to go. Why do you ask?"

"That's why I was in the hallway. I was coming to your office. I think we still need the continuity that you bring to the program; and I don't want to miss something that we may not have been exposed to. So, I am requesting that you attend the meeting with us."

"OK, I'll have my assistant get right on it."

"Thank you, Mel. See you later."

I attended the project meeting, along with about 300 other Lockheed Martin and Air Force personnel. I suspect, 299 people in that room did not realize that I was the only person of color in attendance; and if the program manager had not asked me to attend, there would have been none. I was not uncomfortable in this environment because I was placed in similar situations quite frequently, as in other program meetings or boarding a flight. I often thought, how would "they" feel if matters were reversed, being the only Anglo in a room or on a flight with all people of color?

As we began to build and test the second unit more and more money was diverted to Bosnia. Finally, the day came when we got the word to start shutting down the program. The unit was about 90 – 95% complete when we got the word. It was my job to assure proper shut down of the program and storage of the unit. I remember very well the month in which the final shutdown occurred. It was in December, and I already had a vacation planned to take the family back home to L.A. So here it was, I'm scheduled to leave for vacation and I didn't know if I had a job when I came back. To make matters worse, the company was deeply in the lay-off cycle that I had foreseen, so I didn't know what to expect. Current employment was down 5000 to around 11,000. Before I left to go on vacation, the Quality Director called me into his office.

"Mel, you did a great job for us on Brilliant Pebbles. Go, take your vacation and don't worry about your job back here. We'll have something on your return."

That was great to hear, however, I knew the company. If things changed, it would not have been the first time that a director would have to go back on their commitment. We went on vacation and what I do remember was that it was one of the best vacations that we ever had. Went skiing on Dez's birthday, a couple of late-night movies, Disneyland, a party at Renee's Mom and Dad, etc.

Nephew moving to Orlando

We lived in Orlando for about a year when my nephew, Keith, asked if he, his wife, and daughter could move in with us. After some discussion Renee and I agreed. Keith felt that L.A. and all of its distractions would not be a good environment for his family. I couldn't argue since that same conclusion started us on our odyssey. We made plans that we would bring his family out over the Christmas holiday. His wife would use my return ticket (this was before 9/11 and the airlines were much more lenient on ticket transfers) and I would help Keith drive his car back to Orlando. I knew it took m e and Renee's dad 64 hours for my original trip, so I added another eight hours, just in case. I was timing the trip so that I could be home watching the college games on New Year's Day. I also knew that on the first trip, I had an eight-hour rest stop for Renee's dad at my friend Gil's home in Houston, Texas. I figured I had 16 hours of margin to play with.

    We started our trip about five AM, with me behind the wheel, and got on Rte. 10 or the Santa Monica freeway that would turn into the San Bernardino freeway. We would be on this one highway, across the entire country, all the way to Florida to Rte. 75. Once we got to rte. 75, we would head south to Orlando. We were on the road for about 45 minutes when I noticed the engine was running rough and skipping. I asked Keith when was the last time the car had been checked? He said he had taken it to the shop only a few days earlier, to be checked out, specifically for this trip. Well, I knew we were going to burn a lot of gas and possibly not make it to Orlando the way this car was running. Fortunately, I had worked on cars before (this was pre-computerization) and had some idea of what the problem was. We pull off Rte. 10 and looked for an auto supply store (since there was no Google, we had to manually drive up down several streets). We found several auto supply stores, but none would open before 7:00 AM. We pulled into the closest one to the highway and waited. Cars had computers in them, but not like the computers of 2019. We changed out the distributor cap and spark plug wires with the ones we bought. By now it was about 7:45. We are only an hour into the trip and already two hours behind.

    We are cruising through the high desert of California, with me still driving, as we approached the city of Barstow. Suddenly, I felt a little jerk in the steering wheel. There were some big rigs on the road and we had been passing them with regularity. When I felt the little jerk, I slowed down from 70 mph to about 60 mph and got in the right-hand lane. I didn't want to have an accidental encounter with one of those big rigs we frequently passed or one going in the opposite direction. After about another five minutes I felt another jerk, this one more noticeable than the first. On the second instance, I began to look for an exit. An exit was coming up, one mile ahead. I slowed way down, flashers on, and prayed. Just as we got off the highway and coming down the exit ramp, the left front ball bearings gave out and the wheel came off the hub. This could have been catastrophic had this happened at high speed on a crowded highway. It was about 3:30 PM. We both get out of the car and look at the damage.

"Well, it's obvious that we are not going anywhere until we get this thing repaired," I said.

We could see more buildings in one direction than the other.

"It looks like there are more buildings in that direction, so why don't I get started walking." Keith said.

So, Keith set out to see if he could find an auto repair shop. I stayed with the car since everything that he owned was in it. About a half hour later Keith returns, riding in a pick-up. The driver gets out, looks at the car and says,

"I have to make a delivery, when I get back, we can go to the salvage yard and pick up a replacement hub. Doesn't look like there is any other damage. When I return, I'll have the tow truck and I'll take you to the shop."

The mechanic returns about an hour later. "Let's get your car off the road, to my shop, then we'll make the run to the salvage yard."

The guy was really nice. But he also knew we were not in a very good position to negotiate, so I didn't know when the nice guy would turn bad guy. Once we dropped the car off, Keith and the mechanic went to the salvage yard. If you do the math, you will realize it was about 5:30 PM when Keith and the mechanic left to go to the salvage yard. This trip also took about a half hour. Problem was, the salvage yard closed at 5:00 PM. Instantly, I didn't like the ramification of this news. Now you would think that the mechanic, who lives in the town, deals with the salvage yard on a regular basis, would know when the salvage yard would close.

"Would a parts supply house, that stays open later have the part that we need?" I asked

"I don't think so, but I'll make a few calls."

He came back shaking his head. Oh boy, that meant that we would have to stay the night.

"What time does the salvage yard open?"

"Well, that is one good thing, they open at 7:00 AM."

Keith and I stayed with the car. It was a long night as I could never go to sleep sitting up. Couldn't wait until 7:00 AM. Let's see, three hours just outside of L.A. and hmmm, maybe 17 hours here, getting home to watch football seems to be getting away from me. That night I looked up in the sky and saw a plane fly overhead. I thought, that could be the flight that Renee, Lana, and Ebony are on, relaxed comfortable, "the easy way to fly." Me, I'm tired, cold, trying not to be disappointed, or jump on Keith about the condition of his car. I tried to look at the bright side, we didn't have an accident or worse. Finally, 7:00 AM came, along with the mechanic. He and Keith took off again to make the trip to the salvage yard. This time they returned with the needed part. The part and labor were about $125. You may not think this as being very much, but this was when gas was under $.75 and minimum wage was about $2.75. The mechanic only wanted cash. Keith pulled money from his pocket, $75 and some change. He looked at me. I made up the balance. We got on the road, 20+ hours behind schedule and not even out of the state of California.

We made it across Arizona, then New Mexico. Believe me I was counting every mile as a victory. I was driving (again) when we entered Texas and I noticed that the engine was starting to run hot. I looked in the rear-view mirror and saw that a little smoke was coming out of the tailpipe. I began to check the signs to see when we would be coming up to a service station or small grocery store. After about a mile, I saw a sign, "Gas/ Food," two miles ahead. As it turned out, the place had two pumps and about 100 items in the store. A can of oil was twice the price a person would expect to pay. I checked the oil, 1 ½ quarts low. I bought a quart and asked how far down the road is the next gas station. It was New Year's Eve so there were not a lot of stores or stations opened. In fact, the owner said he was going to be closing in an hour or two. However, he did say that there was one 10 miles behind us and one about 20 miles ahead of us. Big decision. I opted to buy another quart of oil and set sight on the one 20 miles ahead. When we got to the gas station, we checked the oil again. At the rate the engine was consuming oil, I figured we could go about 175 miles to every quart. The oil at this stop was half again as much as a person would expect to pay. Still, the price of the oil was too much for us to buy any significant quantity. We bought another quart for safety and determined that as soon as we get to a big city, we would buy a case of oil.

Keith took over driving for a few hours until about 9 PM, at that time I took over driving again. It was just after midnight, in the middle of nowhere, in the state of Texas where only the buffalo roam, I was thinking of the football games I was going to miss. It was a clear night, no moon, just the stars, with a faint glow of a fairly large city in the distance. As I came over a slight rise, that city that I had noticed earlier was momentarily blacked out. It's late at night, now New Year's Eve, am I hallucinating, have I been driving too long? I don't know what it was that blocked out the city, but I began to move into the right-hand lane of the divided highway. I was traveling about 70 mph and began to slow down a little bit, when suddenly, a man wearing a dark overcoat appeared in the headlights. He was walking in the road, in the left-hand lane. Had I not began moving over when I did, and began slowing down, I would have hit this guy traveling at 70 miles per hour. As it was, I barely missed him. Keith, day dreaming or cat napping, responded to the sudden jerking of the car. He sat up and said,

"What was that?"

"It was a guy walking down the middle of the road, drunk. I hope he gets home 'cause he has another part of the highway to cross."

This was one of those times when I wanted to do something, but was unsure of what to do. It is said that no action is action. Maybe my action on this occasion was not the best choice. I don't know. I do know that my instincts saved me from killing the guy. I moved over and slowed down. Keith himself said that he was glad that I was driving that patch of road that night. We drove all of New Year's Day with me listening to whatever game we could catch on the radio. That evening we pulled into Tallahassee and gave Renee a call. We were still eight hours, maybe 10 hours away from home. We bought another case of oil, the second case, as the car was now burning about a quart every hour. When we finally made it home, exhaustion was not the word. I had about six – eight hours sleep in four days. Remember, it only took 64 hours or two and a half days for my father-in-law and I to drive the same route, including an eight-hour layover in Houston.

New Assignment

When I came back from Christmas vacation, I began the task of shutting down the Brilliant Pebbles program. It was a sad day when I rolled the BP unit into a secured room and placed a padlock on the door. Afterwards, for about eight months, I was on "Special Assignment" working with other programs providing assistance where needed. Mostly, I helped develop proposals since I had a finance background and now had a fairly good understanding of Quality. One day the Quality Director asked if I would be interested in a temporary assignment working on the "East Side." The job would be about a month and would begin the first Tuesday after Labor Day. Since there was not much happening on the "West Side," I took the offer. Besides, the company was down to about 8,000 employees now.

That Tuesday I reported in to Gary, the Quality Director, and received my assignment. It was a 30-day project and I would be finished by the first week of October. Sometime during the second week, Gary called me into his office.

"Mel, I like your work, the experience, and sanity that you bring to the group. Would you be willing to stay on for a few more weeks?"

"Gary, that's not a very difficult decision, there isn't much to go back to on the West side."

As it turned out, I worked with Gary for 12 months. I had not been at the facility for very long when Gary asked me to perform an audit on a Boeing Helicopter Test Equipment area. Boeing had been in the facility about four months before and the area performed very poorly. I began my investigation and found 21 significant problems that needed correction. I compiled my findings in a notebook. In the notebook, I stated what the findings were, what regulation(s) was violated, what needed to be done to correct the finding, and when the finding was to be corrected.

Having been through so many Government audits, and being the Program Manager of Total Quality Management, I was probably best suited to help resolve the issues, even though I had written the findings. I began to help the areas correct the problems and was up to number 16 when a strange thing happened. I was walking down the hall and passed one of the small conference rooms. Just as I came parallel to the room, a Martin Marietta project manager, in the Boeing Test Equipment area, came out the door.

"Mel, I was just going to come get you. Do you have your book where you did the audit and corrective action on our area?"

Now this is what was strange. I had the book in my hand. To this day, I had no idea why I had the book or where I was going with the book. When he asked me if could come in the meeting with him, I didn't say that I had to go to another area or another meeting, I just said;

"Oddly enough, I have the book with me. Why?"

"Boeing is here and we would like for you to present your findings and corrective action that you have done to date."

"OK, sure."

I was introduced to the four-member Boeing team and was asked to talk about the findings and corrective actions that I had in my notebook. After about an hour and a half, I was up to about number 12 when the Lead guy from Boeing asked;

"Are the remaining four as detailed as the previous ones?"

"Yes, they are. I would be willing to make a copy for your later review if you are running short on time."

"It is not that we are running short on time. Since we have been coming here, we have not seen an audit documented so well, the corrective action identified so clearly, and implementation and follow-up so well done; that I don't think we need to sit and have you go through the rest of them. There were 21 findings, you have completed 16, will those remaining five be as thorough as the first 16?"

"Without question."

The Boeing lead looks at the Lockheed Martin Test Equipment Manager (TEM).

"Will Mel continue to be on the project to complete the corrective action?"

"Of course, Mel will be responsible to get you the final document." The Project Manager said.

I interjected and said, "You will receive a copy of the final report and all documentation.".

The Boeing lead then looked at the TEM assembly area.

"I came here prepared to shut down the program. However, and because of the work that Mel has done, I will put your program in a 'Yellow' classification, meaning that it will be under surveillance. There is also one condition, you have Mel continue his work and send copies of his report to us. If he comes off the project before he completes the corrective active process, then I will be forced to shut the program down."

The TEM assured Boeing that I would stay on the project and that they would get copies of my documentation. Then the Boeing lead asked if all of the Lockheed Marin team would leave the room.

"Do you mind if we have some time to ourselves to discuss what has been presented?"

"Uh, sure. We can all leave." The TEM said.

Then the Boeing lead did something unprecedented and very unusual. As I got up to leave. , ,

"Mel, would you mind staying?" He asked.

I looked at the TEM. He nodded his head.

"Sure, I'll stay."

Mind you, what the Boeing representative asked was unprecedented. It is not unusual for the Program Manager of the area to stay and speak with the Customer alone, but not one of the team members. The Program Manager is ALWAYS in attendance on any discussion involving his program. So, to ask him to be one of the ones to leave is unheard of. The Boeing lead was just so impressed with the work that I had done that he wanted to know where I came from and why this division had not had me participate in previous audits. I told them my background of being a Quality Business Manager, Quality Manager, Program Lead for the new Government Quality program, and Company Program Manager on Total Quality Management (TQM).

"Oh yea, I forgot, also was lead for the Baldrige Award that we received, and ISO 9000."

The Boeing Manager said, "No wonder. Well, we are impressed. I hope this company realized how much money and energy you saved them. As I said I came with orders to shut the program down. But with your documentation, I'm sure my management will agree to the 'Yellow' condition I put the program in. To reopen a program is a three-month process, minimum. None of us wanted that. So, for three months they would not have been able to ship any hardware; and, they would have to prove that all findings had been corrected. Personally, I'm glad that I met you and on my next visit I want you on the roster to give us an update."

We shook hands and I went back to inform Gary, the Quality Director of what had just happened.

"I am surprised. I didn't even know they were here. We should have been informed," he said. Anyhow I told him what happened and that we averted a program shutdown.

"Mel, I am glad you were here with us and that you were on that project. I will let the company President know what happened and that you were able to avert a program disaster and shutdown. A couple of days went by when Gary and I were talking abut some program issues when he voluntarily expressed his anger.

"Mel, I just don't understand it. I have been holding this back for a couple of days now. Had anyone else did what you did with Boeing they would have received a bonus, an award and who knows what else. I understand that nothing has been said to you?"

"No, nothing has been said."

"That is unfortunate, especially for the money and manpower you saved this Company."

"Gary, unfortunately, it has not been unusual for this company to overlook my contributions, many of which have been extremely significant."

I told Gary of some of the other things that I had done without recognition or reward.

"Well, we will make sure you get something. May not be as big as it should be, but we'll figure something out."

Personally, I was disappointed but not surprised that, once again, I encountered "**A Glass Unbroken**."

Gary meant well, but nothing ever happened. It was one of those OBE (overtaken by events) things as we were busy fighting other fires.

"Civilians don't often appreciate nor reward leadership, innovation, or dedication. The service does and has recognized innate leadership in you; which, will not necessarily be so in the civilian sector where politics and envy can come into play." General Olds.

The Gulf War

I had the fortunate experience of contributing to the 1991 Gulf War that may never be known except by this writing. At the onset of the Gulf War, the United States continuously sought to keep Israel out of the war while Iraq sought to bring Israel into the war by launching SCUD missiles at Israeli population centers. It just so happened that the facility in which I was working was assembling the launch and test equipment for the Patriot missile, otherwise known as the "SCUD Buster." The U.S. was shipping the Patriot missiles to Israel and setting up a self-defense perimeter around the cities. For some unknown reason, the launch vehicles began to fail during testing. There were several toggle switches on the vehicles that would not pass the testing temperature range of 140F to -40F. Since the launch vehicles were not passing testing, we could not ship the Patriots to Israel for their self-defense, increasing the likelihood of Israel getting involved in the war. The sub-systems that were failing were being built by a company in Florida which was about 100 miles from our facility. Gary asked me to accompany four other engineers as they went to the company to try and determine what was wrong. We had packed bags for four days, since we had no idea what to expect. When we arrived at the facility, they marched us into a conference room and began to give us a presentation of what they believed may be causing the failure. It was Greek to me. I was antsy. I began to fidget, so much so that our lead engineer noticed.

"Mel, what's the problem?" I knew Tom fairly well and in fact we made the drive together, so I was comfortable in speaking my mind.

"Tom, sitting here is not going to help us. We need to get out on the manufacturing floor. I need to see their process and see what they may be doing wrong."

Tom looked at me, trying to assess the importance of what I said and the breach in protocol that I was suggesting. Finally, he made up his mind.

"I hate to interrupt your presentation, it is in fact quite informative, however, I have to yield to a request by our Quality Manager (Yeah right, blame it on me). He wants to spend time on the factory floor, to better understand your process, prior to seeing a presentation. He thinks it would give us better understanding of the equipment and how it goes together."

With that the meeting broke up and we went to the factory floor. The loosely held respect between Engineering and Quality seems to be the same no matter where you go. This was a quality issue, and yet their Quality Manager (QM) was not in the meeting. Neither was the QM with us as we toured the factory. In fact, all the engineers were talking amongst themselves as we began to separate. I'm not sure how much they were actually looking at the assembly process, but I sure was. We had been in the factory for just over an hour when I noticed a particular operation. I was walking alone. I stopped and just stood there to watch. It was about five minutes when Tom realized I was not only with the group but couldn't be seen; Tom showed up and stood next to me.

"I wondered where you went to. Do you see something?" Tom asked.

"Not sure, but I believe so. Do you see how she is testing the toggle switch, the metal contact plate?"

"I am looking, but I don't see what it is that she is doing wrong."

It wasn't too long before all the other engineers realized that Tom was no longer with them, but was standing next to me. It didn't take them very long to join us. I'm sure the young lady we were watching was starting to get really nervous, having about 10 people watching her work, along with several senior managers. I continued to watch, while there was a building buzz behind me, wondering what we/ I was looking at.

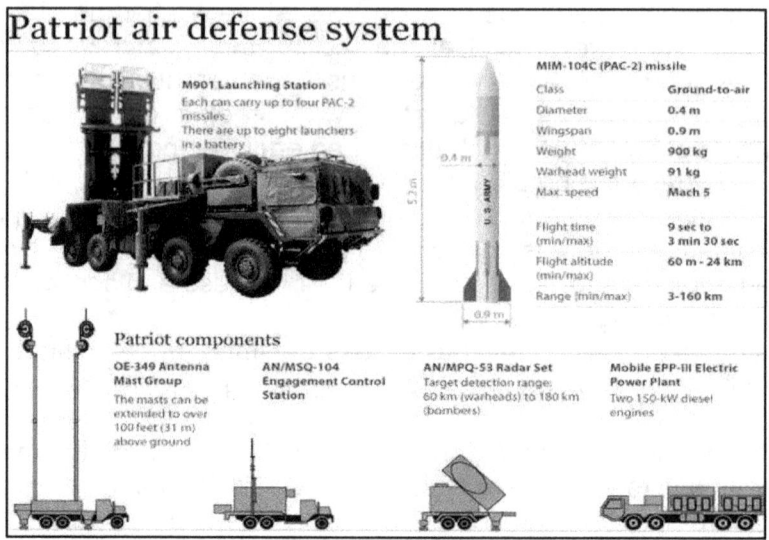

I turned to the group and asked, "How is she testing the metal toggle plate?"

One of the engineers said, "She's following the written procedures, so I don't see what's wrong."

I'm sure his comment made the assembler feel much better. Even though she was following procedures, there was something wrong with the procedures.

"Notice how she picks up the metal plate and positions it for continuity, and notice that she is using her bare hands to handle the metal contact?"

"What's wrong with that?" one of the engineers asked.

"Not sure if what she is doing is the culprit, but I have my suspicions. Let's do a control test. Would you mind having her put finger cots on her hand and then repeat the process. My suspicions are that the body oils are coating the metal contact strip."

"You got to be kidding. A little body oil will make that much of a difference?"

"Not sure, but that is what we are going to find out."

We picked 20 toggle switches at random that she had assemble previously and 20 using finger cots. It was about 3:30 in the afternoon, their shift ended at 4:15, so the day was almost gone. We collected the test samples and headed to another area where the toggle switches would be subjected to 140F temperature for a couple of hours then taken to a chiller for four hours. We estimated that it would be about 1:00 AM before the units would be ready to test. This project was of such importance that none of us hesitated about staying and performing the test, regardless of the hour. Once the unit got into either the heater or chiller, we would be able to go get something to eat. We came back to the facility around midnight, and waited the final hour. The control group of 20 (the ones assemble without finger cots) were tested and only one passed testing. This was a 5% acceptance rate which was totally unacceptable. We then tested the remaining 20; the ones assembled using finger cots. The engineers were amazed. We had 100% acceptance.

"You mean to tell me body oil made the difference?"

"It would appear to be so. I would recommend using either gloves or finger cots for all assemblers and testers in your factory."

"Amazing. Don't worry, it will be done. Done tomorrow." The Lead Engineer said.

Tom came up to me, "Mel, we would not have noticed that in a million years. We obviously were prepared to be here for several days if not longer. I just can't get over the fact that you were able to pick that out. That's why you wanted to get to the factory floor and not sit in the briefing. Good move.

"Tom, I used to be an Industrial Engineer, were I practically lived on the floor. That's why I wanted to come out to the production area."

"Well, let's go get some sleep and we'll brief their management team in the morning."

That following morning, we briefed their management team on our findings and corrective action. They too were dumbfounded but graciously accepted our recommendation of either gloves or finger cots for the factory area. Before we left, they began to assemble a launcher sub-assembly with the toggle switches we had tested the night before. A couple of days later, one of those sub-assemblies went into a Launcher that was loaded with four Patriot missiles, which in turn was loaded into a C5A, cargo plane; and, within 24 hours after having arrived in Israel, one the Patriots intercepted a SCUD. Although I received recognition from the engineers in which I accompanied on this trip, the senior management team of Martin Marietta failed, once again, to recognize my effort and the potential catastrophe that was averted.

"Civilians don't often appreciate nor reward leadership, innovation, or dedication. The service does and has recognized innate leadership in you; which, will not necessarily be so in the Civilian sector where politics and envy can come into play." General Olds.

Activities

In October 2012, while living in Pennsylvania, Renee and I went to visit the old neighborhood, stopping in to see Ed, Carol and a couple of other neighbors. As Ed and I were talking, catching up on what has happened to one another since the last time we visited, he stopped talking, looked at me and said, "The neighborhood hasn't been the same since you and Renee left. You guys were so generous, truly an example of how God's love is supposed to be. We really miss you." He went on to talk about how there was always something happening at the King's; and, that no matter what was happening, they knew they were invited to come. He went on and spoke about the football games in our backyards, the impromptu pool parties, bar-b-que, the basketball games in the Lister's driveway, and a host of other activities. Oh, can't forget the water-gun fights. We were always doing something fun.

Surprise Birthday Party

Sometime before we left Orlando, Renee gave me a surprise birthday party and flew Gary, one the TV crew members from Crenshaw Christian Center, out for the event. Gary and I are good friends so this was Renee's payback from her 40th birthday party. Phil, Gary, Troy, and Doug collaborated in a song and dance routine that I'm sure would have gone viral on the internet of today. The day following, we went to a friend's house that lived on a lake in north Orlando. A group of us were there, playing volleyball, water skiing, and tubing (inner tube being pulled by boat). I think Gary had the most fun since it was so new to him. The object of tubing is to hold on for dear life as the boat driver attempts to de-throne you. You either hold on and stay upright for five minutes or get dunked, whichever comes first.

A Satellite Launch

Since I worked at Martin Marietta, I was able to get VIP parking for the company rocket launches or for shuttle launches. On one occasion, my sister Vic, my son Aaron and our neighbor's son, Eddie, went to go see a company launch. We were about a mile and a half from the launch site, with loud speakers around providing input about the launch. Aaron and Eddie, being young boys and doing what young boys do, were wrestling, playing tag, and hardly paying any attention to what was happening, that is until the count-down started. When the count-down started, the two boys abruptly stop their playing and very discretely put the car in between them and the launch vehicle. The action was unspoken between them, but both acted concurrently. When the vehicle launched, the night sky was turned into daylight. Had we wanted to, we very easily could have read a newspaper. The sound was tremendous. It was awesome.

A few months later, Aaron's teacher gave an assignment to the class to discuss a current event. One news story was that the space shuttle was being launched to correct a programing problem on a satellite. It was front page news. It just so happened that this satellite was carried aloft by the same launch vehicle that I had taken Aaron and Eddie to see. With my knowledge of what happened, and the fact that Aaron was there for the launch, he was able to give an in-depth, and rousing report.

"Me, my dad, my Auntie Vic, Eddie, Eddie is one of my best friends, well we had this opportunity to go to Cape Canaveral and watch a real live satellite launch. There were a lot of people around and cars were parked everywhere. They had loudspeakers that told us what was happening. At first me and Eddie, uh Eddie and I were playing around wrestling and stuff until we heard the countdown on the loudspeaker. We looked at each other and without a word, we both decided that we were going to put the car between us and the rocket. The rocket was only a couple of miles away, and it was all lit up. But we didn't know if it was going to blow up, or what it was going to do. All I know is, I know what bottle rockets can do, and this was a much bigger rocket. (The class laughed at this analogy). We heard the count down, 'three...two...one. We have ignition. We have lift-off'

This was at night and it was dark. But when that rocket started up in the air, it lit the whole night. It was like the sun had come out. We watched it go up and up and up. We must have watched it five or ten minutes. It was Aw-w-some."

"Well Aaron, great story and what a terrific experience, but what does that have to do with your current event assignment?"

"That's the neat part. Astronauts on yesterday's shuttle launch are going up to repair a satellite that didn't go into orbit. Well, that satellite is the same satellite that we saw being launched that night. Besides, my dad told me why it didn't go into orbit. You see, only one satellite was on board the rocket, and it was in the second of two cargo bays. Since there was no satellite in the first cargo bay, the software was not programed to search for a satellite in the second bay. Since there was none in the first bay, the software shut down and did not attempt to launch the satellite in the second cargo bay. The satellite was pushed out of the launching rocket, but the booster to get it to go to orbit never got the command to ignite. So, it just floated there. And now, the astronauts are going up to strap on a booster rocket to get it into its proper orbit; which, is on the front page of the Orlando Sentinel. And that is my report." Aaron got an A+.

Shuttle Launches

One day I told Mr. M, the school principal, that I could get passes to see a shuttle launch. He thought a moment and then said, "Great, I can use that for my eighth graders and others as a reward." We had an eight-passenger custom van, decked out with CD, video player, and a TV. Mr. M would drive the van and he gave Aaron the honor of selecting two of the places in the van. Needless to say, when it was known that a trip to Cape Canaveral was coming up, everybody was nice to Aaron.

Mr. M was a great principal and even today we still consider him and his wife, friends.

At the Airport prior to 911

While at my temporary assignment to the East facility, there was an opportunity for Lockheed Martin to bid on a contract. The proposal office is in Cherry Hill, NJ. I am asked to go and be the Quality lead for the proposal. The assignment is going to be about six weeks. I show up at the program office on a Thursday and I am immediately put to work. I am at the office for two solid weeks, including the weekends. Finally, I get word that I am able to leave at noon Friday to go home for the weekend.

I book a flight out of Philly, which so happens to be a puddle jumper to New York, then its non-stop from New York. I arrive at the Philly Airport. No plane. I am waiting in the boarding area for an hour and a half, when it is finally announced that a plane will be available. I board the plane, knowing that my connection in New York is now in jeopardy. We land at the Kennedy airport. We are on the tarmac, not at one of the terminals. A bus pulls up alongside the airplane and waits. As soon as the "buckle your seatbelts" sign goes off, the aisle is crammed with passengers. As soon as the doors open, an airline representative enters the plane and yells out, "Will Passengers Mel King and Joe Smith, please come to the front. I need you both to come with me immediately." My first thought was 'What did I do?' Her actions were highly unusual for an airline. Both of us were near the back of the plane and people had already jammed the aisle, so there wasn't much we could do. However, this lady was persistent.

"Please listen up. I need you to clear the aisle. I need to have Mel King and Joe Smith come with me immediately." She spoke in a voice and manner that was very authoritative. The Red Sea parted. Joe (whom I didn't know) and I got our belongings and walked off the plane and unto the waiting bus.

The rep said, "I was asked by the airline to pull you off as quickly as possible. You have a small window to get to your connecting flight. It is highly unusual what they are doing; however, I am pleased to help you get to where you are going."

About seven or eight other passengers who were in the front of the plane had gotten on the bus. When the rep got on the bus and saw the others she said, "This bus is for King and Smith. There will be another bus for you. You all will have to get off and wait for the other bus."

"Is this bus going to the same terminal as the other bus that is coming?" I asked.

"Yes, it is," the rep said.

"Then why not let them stay on. It will take longer for them to get off than if they stayed on the bus. We can leave now if they stay on."

"Makes sense. Let's go," she said to the driver.

I think the driver must have driven a cab before this job. He did us well.

We arrived at the terminal, ran up the stairs and ran up to the security check-in. (This is prior to 911. Bags were screened but there were no lines to check identity or boarding passes. The only line was for the X-ray machines.) The line was long for the baggage check.

"Well let's see if we can get you to the front of the line. Come on," the rep said.

As we got to the front, there was this gentleman, about 6'5", 280lbs+ (reminded me of Big Foot) was at the head of the line.

"Pardon me sir, if you don't mind, I need to get these two gentlemen through," the rep said.

The man acted as if he didn't hear her and continued to put his belongings in the bins.

The rep repeated herself, "Pardon me sir, if you don't mind, I need to get these two gentlemen through."

Joe and I each had one carry-on. I grab his bag tossed it on the rack and followed quickly with mine. They disappeared into the machine. Big Foot was so indignant that he began to turn red. We didn't stay around for the explosion. We met our bags on the other side of the X-ray machine.

"Mel, your gate is about 10 gates down, Joe's gate is in another area."

"OK, you stay with Joe, I'll go to my gate by myself. Thanks for your help. Bye"

I'm off and running, doing the OJ thing, when doing the OJ thing in airports was OK. I get to my gate and I'm hearing this alarm going off.

"Hi I'm here for my flight to Orlando," I said.

"Hear that bell, that means the plane has left," The check-in rep said.

"Is that the plane that I'm looking at?"

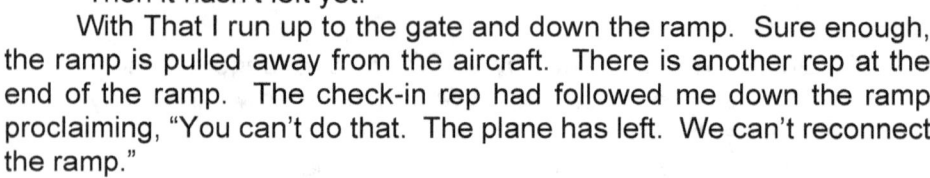

"Yes, it is."

"Then it hasn't left yet."

With That I run up to the gate and down the ramp. Sure enough, the ramp is pulled away from the aircraft. There is another rep at the end of the ramp. The check-in rep had followed me down the ramp proclaiming, "You can't do that. The plane has left. We can't reconnect the ramp."

So now there are three of us looking at the plane. Meanwhile, I see the pilot going through his checklist.

"Can you re-connect the ramp to the aircraft?" I asked.

"Not without the pilot's permission," the rep said.

I looked around the ramp and saw a black phone.

"Does that phone connect to the pilot?"

"Yes, it does."

"Then please call him and ask for permission to reconnect."

"He won't do that. Technically, he has already left."

"Call him and let him make that decision. Please."

The rep makes the call and I can see the pilot pick up the phone in the cockpit.

"I have a gentleman here that wants to board your aircraft. Do you want to give permission to reconnect?" The attendant says.

The pilot turns to look in our direction, I give him the puppy dog, begging look and he starts laughing. He shakes his head and waves to the rep to bring the ramp back to the plane. The ramp is reconnected, the door opens and I walk through. The flight attendants are surprised.

"Who are you? Are you someone special? Are you someone, somebody we should know?" They asked.

"I am special to my family and the Lord. Other than that, I'm just an average guy," I said. (Maybe a little Uncommon)

"Well, this is a first. Never had the doors opened before, once they were closed, except for an emergency. You are one lucky guy," they said.

"I like to consider myself blessed. But I am glad the pilot made an exception," I responded.

When we landed in Orlando, I saw the pilot and went to thank him.

"Pardon me Sir, I just want to say thank you for letting me on board. I have been away from home for over two weeks, and just have the weekend to see the family. If you hadn't let me on, I would have had to spend the night in New York, and wouldn't arrive here until tomorrow around 10 AM."

"Couldn't resist that puppy dog look. It was my pleasure to do. Enjoy the weekend."

"Again, thank you Sir. Bye."

Safe Harbor

It was August, almost a year later when Gary called me into his office.

"Mel, I have a permanent position available for you if you want it. Because you're not in our division Human Resources (HR) said I would have to post it, interview for it, and a whole bunch of other stuff. Even though I may have to do all that 'stuff,' if you want the position, I am willing to go through all that rigmarole. The position is actually one grade lower than what you are now, but still a manager's position; and, I won't have to touch your salary."

What Gary was offering was a safe harbor. However, Renee and I had been praying about my position with Lockheed Martin (by this time the Company had joined forces with the Lockheed Corporation). The prayer was for an increase in salary and a promotion, not the same salary and a lower position. I was quiet for about a minute as I gathered my thoughts. With reluctance and some dread, but in faith, I responded.

"Gary, my wife and I have been praying about my situation. We have been praying for a promotion and increase. What you have offered doesn't answer our prayers. As much as I like working here; and, especially working for you, Gary, I believe I will have to turn down the offer."

"Well, Mel, I kinda thought you would. But I at least wanted to ask in the off-chance that you said, 'Yes.' You know we really would like to have you. You have done a great job for us here."

"Thanks again Gary for the offer. And, I am deeply grateful that you didn't try to make the decision for me, by deciding that I would say 'No' and not even make the offer. Thank you."

With that, there was nothing more to be said. I got up to leave.

"Please close the door as you leave, I need to finish some work. Thanks again, Mel."

As I pulled the door shut and heard the faint "click," it sounded like two monstrous doors being shut with absolute finality "BAM." I just closed the door on a safe harbor. I had to believe that I was in the safe harbor of the Lord's hands. However, I couldn't help thinking about all the things that I had done for this division and the total lack of recognition. Why is that Glass ceiling so prevalent?

One week after Labor Day, on a Tuesday, I was sitting in my office fretting over a couple of rumors that I heard. By this time, the company was down to 4,000 employees (from a high of 16,000). As a result of the reduction in employees, not as many managers were needed. The solution, reduce the number of managers. The rumors were that a reduction in grade level was coming and a corresponding reduction in salary. So, I'm sitting at my desk fuming, and thinking.

"Now I'm going to get a reduction in grade level and also a reduction in pay. Humph, shoulda taken that job on the east side, at least I would not have had my pay cut."

I was getting more upset by the minute. Suddenly I heard this still quiet voice.

"Do you trust me?"

I put my pen down sat back in my chair and got quiet mentally and physically.

"Do you trust me?"

Instinctively I knew it was Holy Spirit asking me about my faith.

"Of course, I trust you. You know I do. You saw me turn down that job offer. It could have been a safe haven for me. I really went out on a limb."

"Do you trust me?"

"Yes, Lord."

"Then why are you fretting?"

"Why am I fretting? You hear what they want to do. They not only want to reduce me in grade but also reduce my salary. Don't I have a right to fret?"

"Do you trust me?"

"Yes Lord!"

"Then trust me."

After several moments of soul searching, I said, "I do and I will."

With that exchange I was a different person, so much so that I was not aware of the transformation.

As I was sitting at my desk, one of my co-workers walked by, looked in at me, stopped, backed up, and said, "Mel, you looked like you just swallowed a Cheshire cat. What are you grinning about?"

I had no idea that what happened to me on the inside had manifested itself on the outside. I told him that a private thought had come to mind and I was still amused by it. He just chuckled and walked away. I was more joyous than ever. Had my co-worker walked pass my office a minute earlier, he would not have seen a Cheshire cat but a sour puss. Glory be to the Lord.

An Interview

Two days later, on a Thursday, I get a call from a Lockheed VP whose office is in Valley Forge, PA. He said that he was looking at my resume and wanted to speak with me about a new position. This position would be in a brand-new division. The division was created to handle all of Lockheed Martin's computers, messaging, and Information Technology systems. The position the VP wanted to fill was a senior manager responsible for all 80,000+ desktop and 20,000 level II computers in the whole company, along with associated software. The position would also report directly to him, a Vice President.

The Word – Deliverance

Before leaving Orlando for good, I spent six months living in an apartment near King of Prussia, PA, and flew back to Orlando every other weekend for business meetings and family visits. One Friday morning I was at the Philadelphia airport waiting to catch a plane to Orlando, it was an eight o'clock flight. The day was very cold, and it was snowing. About 45 minutes before departure, the attendant at the check-in counter made an announcement that our plane was going into the hangar for repairs and we would all have to take a later flight, the earliest of which was around 1:30 PM. This was not good. I was scheduled to leave at noon with Renee to go to a Benny Hinn crusade near Fort Lauderdale. Aaron and Dez were going to be staying with some friends. It's about two hours flying time from Philly to Orlando, so any flight after 9:15 meant that I would not be able to drive down to Fort Lauderdale in time for the start of the Crusade.

I prayed about the situation and the need of getting to Orlando on time.

"Lord, there must be a reason why this challenge has risen. I won't give Satan credit for knowing the future; however, I do know he will try to put obstacles in our path when we want to, and are serving you. He knows I want to get to Fort Lauderdale, and is trying to not make that happen. I am believing that I will be able to get there, get there on time, and it shall be to your glory."

Another 10 minutes passed when the attendant made an announcement.

"The plane that is/ was supposed to take you to Orlando was scheduled to go to the hanger because the coffee machine is not working. The aircraft is functional and is airworthy. The pilot asked me to ask all of you if you still wanted to go to Orlando; however, without a working coffee maker? It would mean that you will not have any coffee on the flight."

It was unanimous. Everybody wanted to go, even without the coffee. Once this decision was made, the attendants were now scrambling to get everybody checked-in and on board so they can make an "On-time" departure. They got the utmost co-operation. We settled in on the plane and as we looked out the window, the snowflakes were getting bigger and denser. This doesn't look good. Began praying once again and began to look at each event as a success. Door closed, success. Plane backed away from terminal, success. Plane powered up, success. Pilot guides plane from ramp unto taxi-way, success. In line for take-off, success. On runway, success.

"Attendants, please take your seats for take-off," The Pilot says. Success. Engines whirl up to a throaty roar, success. Breaks release, success. 5. . .10. . 15. . 25. . 30 seconds rotation, front wheels are off the ground, success. We are on our way to Orlando. I was pleased to know that I would be able to drive to Fort Lauderdale with the family. We were in the air for about a half hour when the pilot came on the PA system.

"Thought all of you may be interested in knowing, the Philadelphia Airport has closed due to bad weather. We were one of the last flights to leave. We are in the air now so just sit back and relax. Oh, sorry about the coffee."

Boy were we all glad that we made the decision to fly without coffee. Me, it didn't matter since I don't drink coffee anyway.

Renee and I made it to Fort Lauderdale on time.

During a Benny Hinn Crusade, it is during the Praise and Worship time that many of the healings occur. What is shown on television or what is happening on the platform is a confirmation of the manifested healings. Many of us were focused on the Praise and Worship music and hardly noticed the line of people, waiting to have their healing acknowledged. There were probably in excess of 18,000 people in the arena. This line would be all the individuals that had an issue with their body before they came, but now can physically tell that they no longer have the issue. People would come out of their seat, walk down the steps to the ground floor and get into the line. The line is usually compressed as the ushers try to make sure there is enough room for all who want to come down. Renee and I were on the ground floor, about six rows from the front. Suddenly, I heard a screaming and the rush of many feet. I turned around and saw this young lady, bending over and screaming. What was just as amazing was the empty space around her. She easily had a 15-foot radius of clear space around her, when just a moment before, another body could not have been squeezed in.

People had cleared out, like a drop of soap pushing back the grease in a greasy pan. It happened that quickly.

I got out of my seat, ran over to the young lady. By now she was on her knees. I laid my hands on her head.

"In the name of Jesus, you foul spirit come out of her," I said.

She immediately, stopped screaming, and curled up into a fetal position. Renee came up behind me and began praying and got a modesty blanket and put it over her dress. I continued to lay hands on her when one of the Crusade workers came over.

"What's happening over here? What are you doing?" She asked.

I ignored her as I was focused on the young lady on the floor. At about the same time one of the pastors that travel with Benny also came over. The worker turned around to the pastor and spoke to him.

"This fella is not on the Crusade team and I don't know who he is."

The pastor looked at Renee and then at me.

"I know who he is and the lady is in good hands. Let them be." The pastor said.

"How come I don't know him? I'm supposed to know everyone on the team." She insisted.

"Well now, why don't you just come with me and let them alone. They aren't bothering anybody now. The lady is quiet and is not disrupting the program. Do you want to get her excited and start something? I don't think you want to do that. Let it be."

The pastor gently took the worker's arm and led her away. I don't know how much time passed, but the lady came out of her fetal position and just sat on the floor.

"Why am I down here on the floor? What happened? I feel really dizzy." The young lady said.

"Just take it easy. Relax. We are going to stay with you until you feel like you can stand up. Are you here with anyone?" I asked.

"No. I came by myself."

"OK, we are going to get up now. We'll take it slow, but we want you to sit with us. Renee, please go and make sure we have an empty seat next to where we are sitting."

"Can you tell me what happened?"

"I don't remember a thing." The young lady said.

"Don't worry, you'll be OK now," I said.

The young lady sat with us for the rest of the day. She did not remember anything related to the event with her ending up being on the floor.

As she was sitting listening to the Praise and Worship music, she leaned over and said to us; "I have never felt such peace before. My mind just seems so clear."

"Give thanks to the Lord for His peace and grace; and for His deliverance." Renee said.

Transition

Upon acceptance of the position in Valley Forge, we began the process of relocating: informing our friends, the church, and preparing the house for sale. I am starting the new job in November, 1995, but Renee, Aaron, and Dez won't be joining me until June of 1996. For the next seven months I will be flying back and forth to and from Philly.

During the last six months or so, we had a family, Jay, Jen, Jayce, Jenae, Jesse and David stay with us. We had known them for a couple of years and their children became close friends with ours. Jay and Jen were aspiring to be pastors and to acquire a home. Their staying with us permitted them to save enough money to put a down-payment on a home in the area of Altamonte Springs in northeast Orlando. Our home had five bedrooms so it didn't feel crowded. Jay & Jen had the downstairs bedroom with the pool bath, Jayce and David stayed in Aaron's room, Jenae and Jessie had the other remaining bedroom. Dez was in her own bedroom. Since they all went to the same school, Renee would take everyone in our Chevy custom van at the same time. The van could sit eight, with luggage space behind the seats to carry small bags. Prior to leaving for school, Renee and Jen would have the kids form an assembly line. Each child would have their spot, bread, mayonnaise, mustard, lettuce, bologna, wrapping, chips, cookies, and finally all stuffed in a brown lunch bag. The Brady Bunch had nothing on us.

While on assignment on the Eastside, I purchased a Pontiac Sunfire. I would need this car in Valley Forge, so it was necessary to plan a weekend when Renee and I would drive the car up and she would fly back to Orlando. We made the drive in about 19 hours, stopping for breaks and getting caught in some rush hour traffic along the way. As it turns out, the 19 hours was about the average time for many of the trips that we made between Valley Forge/Downingtown and Orlando. The fastest time was 17 hours (kids sleeping most of the way), the longest time was 21 hours.

Epilogue

As you were reading the assignments I had, the many challenges, and the goals achieved, and in many instances, exceeded expectations, was it strange that I was frequently unrewarded. Many people will go to work and return home without making a significant contribution to the direction or bottom-line of the company of which they work. That wasn't so with me. So, why was there not the recognition? The things I did and accomplished for the company, was I deserving? Was there truly a "Glass Ceiling" in place?

The following comments can only be made, of the things that I was able to accomplish at work, due to the wisdom that the Lord had given. Some things that happened were truly beyond the ordinary; and, the many successes were not typical. Even though Martin Marietta chose not to acknowledge much of what I was able to accomplish, I always had to remember that it was for the Lord in which I was working, not man.

Successes at Lockheed Martin – Orlando

- Provided program chart as a means to more accurately document labor and cost consumption, saving several hundred thousand dollars on multiple programs as company was able to move labor based on need. Company chose to not fully use or implement tool

- Developed a macro driven electronic spreadsheet report that reduced manpower requirement from two people working a full week to one person working half a day

- While as the Quality Business manager, reduced targeted over-run of $14 Mil. to $200 under-run in one year

- Saved another $20 Mil. in cost avoidance by introducing hiring limitations and parameters

- Only one of five Black managers out of 15,000 employees. Being there was not necessarily success on my part, but what was were the many accomplishments, being Black, that I am sure exceeded their expectations.

- Received perfect score for "Cost of Quality" during Government audit

- Re-vitalized poorly performing Quality Cost Control organization, performance improvement of team resulted in numerous promotions and merit increases of team members that were stagnant for over five years.

- Program lead for the successful implementation of the Government **Contractor Performance Certification Program** (CP2), saving both Government and Lockheed Martin millions of dollars. Senior management recognized Importance of program by providing prime rib lunches for entire workforce at beginning of project assessment period and at its successful implementation 18 months later. Government counter-part received a bonus and a promotion, nothing was afforded me.

- Program lead for implementation of **Total Quality Management**, again resulting in significant cost savings. Management Club recognized effort by presenting President's Award. Company never formally recognized accomplishment. However, company had, on its website, that this program was one of the cornerstones for future quality successes.

- Restarted the Quality Newspaper that had been dormant for many years. Received numerous compliments on the improved format and content. (Was originator and chief editor). Subsequent Quality Manager received recognition for production of the newspaper.

- Team lead for Martin Marietta becoming one of the first aerospace companies being awarded the **Baldridge Award**. Company never acknowledged effort to attain this coveted award.

- Insight and knowledge of previous model build avoided major design issues with follow-on Brilliant Pebbles unit. Savings estimated in millions of dollars.

- Was able to maintain a very positive relationship as company coordinator/ liaison with Defense Contract Audit Agency. A non-amiable relationship with this organization can have very negative impact on program audits and unit deliveries.

- Had a direct impact on Gulf War as I was able to determine, in a very short time period (one day) what engineers thought would take, minimum, a week, possibly weeks, what was causing the firing units to fail performance testing. The failures were delaying the shipment of the Patriot launch vehicles to Israel. The units arriving in Israel, along with the Patriot missile, with their capability to destroy the SCUD missile, were critical in minimizing the spread of the Gulf War (1991) to other nations.

- Avoided a complete shutdown by one of our Customer's (Boeing Helicopter) test equipment build area as a result of my experience as Quality Manager and Audit coordinator. A shutdown would have costs the company untold millions in lost labor and revenue. Company President was informed by the Quality Director of the comments of the Boeing team and my actions, avoiding a program shutdown, but President chose to neither reward nor acknowledged my actions.

- Became member and Treasurer of local ASQC (American Society for Quality Control) in support of the Quality director who was President.
    - Received award as "MVP" for local ASQC chapter
    - Later became President of local ASQC chapter

Church Affiliation

Faith Christian Center:

- Help to start church with Pastor James. One of the Elders, ran sound system, performed usher duties and had men's breakfast at our home

Orlando Christian Center:

- School Board Member

- Covenant Couples leadership team member

- Altar Worker leadership team member

- Initiated Men's Fellowship and became first Facilitator

- Coached the girls' soccer team, went to championship game

The following story is an excerpt of one of my childhood adventures

38th Street – The Museum & Rose Garden

It was a warm, dry, kinda hazy day with a very light smog in the City of Angels. We were on patrol and had to provide reinforcement to one of our units that were stranded either in the museum, the rose garden or armory. One of our biggest obstacles was going to be crossing the "Vermont River." This was a wide four-lane boulevard with parking on either side. But to us, it was always the "River." Once we crossed this river, we would be in enemy territory. We had to get across quickly with minimal observation. We had a pre-selected staging point and we gathered to make our forging across the river. We found that when the big barges came down (Semi-trucks with trailers) we were able to run right behind them and have minimal exposure to river traffic. Sometimes it would take a while before one of these barges would appear. But today, we see two barges on the horizon. Our whole squad can probably cross at once. The barges approach and we make ready to move out. One of our new recruits (a new kid that moved into the area) wanted to jump on the barge as it passed by. We nixed that idea. We told him safety was a big thing with us and that we have not ever had any casualties. We told him to wait, and that he would get his share of adventure. Anyhow, crossing the Vermont River was not an easy exercise (it had its dangers). If timing was not right, you had the very real possibility of being struck by river traffic. Well, that day we kept our casualty record intact. We always took pride in not causing any breaks to squeal. Anyone who did cause a break to squeal had to buy a round of bubblegum. We made it across the river and into one of the high buildings to assess our situation. As we deployed to the roof, we took up strategic positions at each corner.

We had some new kids that moved into the neighborhood and they wanted to infiltrate our society. We were open to new members, but first, we had to see what they were made of. This was kind of a trial, to see if they were smart, cool under fire and either quick thinkers or fast learners. We had put these guys into a unit of their own. Told them where we were going and that they had to catch us. We were on the roof waiting. Water grenades in hand.

We were a ragtag group. Some had army helmets, some did not. Some had rifles, some did not. Some had army fatigues (tops only), some did not. Still, we were a formidable force. We got into a number of fights because at our age, we were still playing army. We survived the many fights and the other kids began to respect us. There were times when they, in fact, would join our squad in pursuit of an escaped spy or help us defend headquarters. It wasn't long before we started having drills, training new recruits.

The scouts were set while we evaluated our position and began to rework our next phase of our plan. We had asked the newbies (the new kids) to wait about 10 minutes and then come. Well, it seems like they only waited about five minutes instead. We wanted to be on top of the building to get a lay of the land (it didn't matter that we had done this umpteen time before, it had to be done right). We needed a few minutes to plot our course. We never try to go the same way twice in a row. So, when we saw the newbies on the other side of the Vermont, we adjusted our plan and our schedule. We kept the scouts at the rear two corners (didn't want to have anyone sneak up on us) and had everybody else come forward. Every one picked a target, acknowledged that each target was covered, and then we waited. While they were planning to forge the Vermont, we took note of their tactic, execution and discipline. We were big on discipline. Anyhow, we noticed they gathered in a group, communicated loudly and was totally visible. Not good. To our amazement and horror…they set out amongst the cars and trucks…in the crosswalk. Can you imagine that…using the crosswalk, of all things? Causing the river traffic to come to a halt. Well, after they crossed the Vermont, once again they huddled together and were obviously planning their next move. And again, to our amazement, they walked in a huddle. Straight toward our building. We had a momentary thought of guilt, but that was quickly dismissed. We figured anybody dumb enough to walk together in enemy territory should die together. Water balloon grenades went over the side. A turkey-shoot. Since the newbies were so close together, we held back on some of the grenades. Same effect though.

We drew them into the building by having a scout shoot at them out of the front door of the apartment building. He reluctantly gave ground (as planned) while we made an exit out of the back door. Then the scout began to fire in-between longer and longer intervals. This proved to be unnerving to those under fire and also, during one of the long intervals, provided time for him to make a getaway. The scout caught up to us as we were setting the second ambush. Once again, the scout would be key in making this second operation successful. We had to draw the newbies into the ambush and would use the scout to do it. The scout pretended like he was lost and was looking for us, totally oblivious of the newbie squad sneaking up on him. When the newbie squad got close, the scout feigned surprise and began running. The newbie squad had him in their sights and was not going to let him get away. They began running. We were behind the steps to the main entrance of the museum and in some near-by bushes. They didn't stand a chance. When the scout was up three steps on the stairs, he jumped over the side. The newbies were so intent on the scout that they didn't notice the group of guys in the bushes behind them. Out of the bushes came the grenades. Splat, Splat, Splat. The newbies turned around to ward off the attackers from the bushes. When they did, we came from behind the stairs. Once again, a turkey shoot.

Summer time in Los Angeles or LA as we called it, was hot, not muggy, but still a dip in the water is not a bad thing. That was the only consolation that the newbies had…they were much cooler than the rest of us.

Before we went into the museum, we had to find a place to stash our weapons. We found the bushes around the trees to be a good place for that and is often where we hid them. Afterwards, we did a debriefing on the newbies and pointed out their mistakes. They thought we were generals.

"We hope you learned a few things because now we are going to enter into really hostile territory. The guards in the museum are not friendly, they were at one time, but have become wary of us since the first few visits." Dicky said. (Dicky was the oldest in the group and was the de facto leader).

Mind you, we were never malicious or destructive, the museum just happened to have a lot of exit doors, halls and tunnels (what a great place to hone your evasive skills). As we entered the museum, one of the guards at the main entrance noticed me and then recognized the rest of the gang. He was on his radio immediately. The word was passed along amongst our group.

"We have been identified and the opposing forces are gathering," I said.

We actually wanted to visit the museum a little before we had any encounter with the enemy. But, as is often said, the best laid plans never survive the first contact with the enemy. Well, we immediately implemented our standard SER plan (split, evade and rendezvous). We split into three groups, use evasive tactics for 30 minutes and meet at the rendezvous point. The newbies were ready to leave the museum now and didn't want any part of the guards. We split the newbies up and put them on the more experienced teams. We were off. When we went in three directions the guard at the main entrance knew the "race was afoot." Four other guards quickly joined him and the hunt was on. One guard each went after the two teams but we had the fortune of having two guards.

The guard at the entrance noticed me since I had been to the museum countless of times...and he has attempted to capture me countless of times. He was so desperate to get his hands on me that he even tried to apprehend me one day when I was part of a UN Fact-finding mission (a school trip). He had me in his grasp when the mission leader (the teacher) asked what I had done and if I had broken any law. The guard mumbled something incoherent.

Then the guard said, "Well the last time he was in here...

The mission leader interjected, "the last time he was here? Well, what has he done, today? Has he done anything, today? Did you see him do anything, today?

The guard was perplexed and didn't know how to respond. The mission leader gently pried the guard's hands off my shoulder and stood between me and the enemy.

The mission leader informed him that her students "are not to be manhandled and if there was even a remote chance of that happening again... well...", First time I ever heard the teacher make an incomplete sentence. I was amazed at how quickly the mission leader came to my defense. Wow. As we walked away, I smiled at the guard and winked. Anyhow, I made it a point to be next to the mission leader the whole time thereafter and asked a lot of questions.

But this is another day, and so this day, we (I) had the luxury of having two guards chase me. Mind you, we had never taken or broken anything in the museum, it just slowly evolved into an obsession with the guards to try and capture us. I think they were saying we were disturbing the peace or something like that. Actually, it was a little odd the way these chases occurred. Since we didn't do any damage and had not caused any disturbance prior to the guards coming after us, everything was in slow motion. As long as we didn't run, they couldn't run (disturbing to the other museum guests). So, we learned really quick how to walk really fast. All we needed was to get out of direct line of sight. The problem was they also knew that they had to keep us in direct line of sight. Sometimes these chases would be so intense that we would pass one of our teams and the guards chasing them would pass us right on by. It wouldn't be until the guards came up to the guards chasing us that it would be brought to their attention that they passed us by and a little argument would break out.

"Why didn't you stop those Kids?" One guard would say.

"We didn't know you were chasing them." Another guard would say.

"How could you not know? Did they look like they were looking at the exhibits?" They would fuss.

After all we were walking and not necessarily drawing attention to ourselves. Only a good observer would notice that something was amiss. Anyhow, the argument was our chance. As I said earlier, the museum has a lot of exhibit halls, hallways, exit doors, meeting rooms, storage rooms and all kinds of other places…and I knew most of them, heh, heh. So, exit stage left. We made a left turn went through a small exhibit, made a right turn, went through another small exhibit and there it was, the first entrance to the "underground railroad." The door was half concealed by an exhibit and if a person was not directly in front of it, they wouldn't notice it. We entered. There were four of us. At this point I asked the two newbies to swear to secrecy or they would be left behind. Even Leroy, part of my team, knew that he was about to go where no one on 38th street had gone before. This was my domain. He assured the newbies that even though we were together now, that I could easily loose them. And in the tunnels of the museums there were mummies, snakes, dinosaurs and other things to stoke the hot coals of the mind's imagination. They swore to secrecy. We went through the maze, looked at people who were looking at the exhibits. We frightened a few who saw us or thought they saw something move in the exhibit. The crowds gathered quickly. Those were the most popular exhibits that day. We continued on.

We took some stairs and exited the maze. We were at the miniature train exhibit. This was always fascinating to us, but sometimes the dime cost to get in was beyond our reach. We never took the maze to sneak in to see the trains. If we didn't have the money, we didn't go. Even on this day, we didn't feel right being here, but that was OK, we were just passing through. The two newbies however wanted to stop and watch the trains.

"Hey, can't we just stop here for a few minutes? I've never been in here before."

"No way. That's how you get caught…you can't take your mind off of the objective," I said.

We had about 10 more minutes before we were to meet at the rendezvous. A group of kids about our age were leaving the train exhibit, so we thought we would tag along. I mentioned to the newbies to strike up a conversation with the group. They did and forgot all about the guards. Leroy and I kept a watchful eye out for the guards though. Oh, oh, trouble at two o'clock. Well, they say, when the horse is dead, it's time to get off. We abandoned the group and had about a 25-yard head-start on the guards. Noticing where we were, I knew we were in trouble. We were too far away to the nearest escape hatch. Leroy saw the concerned look on my face. The newbies however didn't notice. They were too mesmerized with how easily we had lost the hunters and gotten around the museum unseen. They didn't realize we were in trouble. I went back to ask the group that we were walking with if they had seen the new dinosaur exhibit. They all became excited and exclaimed that they had not and would just love to see it. I said I couldn't remember where it was but I'm sure those two guards over there would be able to show you. At that, the group was off and running to the guards, all ten of them talking at once. Just as they got the group to quiet down so they could understand them, the guards looked up in our direction. We looked back at the guards as we turned the corner and gave a thumbs up.

At the rendezvous point. All present and accounted for. We went back to the bushes where we had hidden our supplies and made plans for the next leg of our journey. We headed out toward the "Rose Garden" and the Amory.

The Rose Garden was our simulated "live" fire area. Here we practiced our stealth, strategy, and signaling in a manner that is as

realistic as possible. We had the newbies sit on some stairs at the east end of the museum, overlooking the rose garden. This way they would be in an elevated position to see all the action. The rest of us broke into two groups, and went to opposite sides of the rose garden. The Rose Garden is divided into sections where the various types of roses are grown. Walking pathways separate the various sections. The overall dimensions are about 70 yards X 140 yards.

Dicky or I usually gave the pitch to any newbie that moved into the area.

"Well Dicky, do you want to give the pitch or should I?"

"Nah, Mel you give it to 'em, they don't look like they are ready to me."

"Alright, for the sake of you newbies, we are going to go through one of our training exercises. If you want to become part of the group, pay attention, 'cause we will know if you don't. Now the maintenance crew, depending on who is working, will sometimes attempt to get us to leave or chase us out. They know we're doing nothing wrong, but it adds excitement to their day and helps us to get better by being stealthy. We both benefit. Not only will you have to dodge the maintenance crew, you will have to dodge the guys on the opposing team. If seen, they will attempt to shoot you and will shoot to kill. (This last comment got their attention and their more intense focus was apparent). Now you guys sit up here on the steps, watch and learn."

As we walked away, I whispered to Dicky, "Hey Dicky, how'd you like that last comment, huh? Shoot to kill. That really got their attention."

"Yeah, that was a nice touch. OK, let's make it look real. Take your team and we'll see who gets to the other side."

The object of this exercise is to swap ends with as few casualties as possible. Several of us had "Air Rifles." These rifles look fairly realistic. They had a pump action that would compress air so that when the trigger is pulled it made a loud noise, air would come out the front, but it didn't shoot anything. Often times we would stick the barrel in the dirt so when we fired the gun, instead of just air, this big grey cloud would come out the front. It looked very real.

Thus far on this exercise neither team scored a hit. My team was coming up to the pond walkway, which is the widest path and circumnavigates the pond which is in the center of the Rose Garden. The maintenance crew was very active for some reason today. This activity hindered our visibility so to keep from being seen we spent a lot of time crawling from place to place. We had not seen, nor had we been seen by the other team or the maintenance crew. I gave a signal to my team that I would take the point and attempt to cross the pathway first. I was going to take a gamble that Dicky's team was forced to have their head down as much as we had ours. Therefore, instead of crawling, I was going to make a dash to the other side of the path.

I alerted my team that I was ready to run. I gathered my legs under me, took a deep breath, hunkered over, and ran for the other side of the path. Obviously, unbeknownst to me, Dicky was on the other side of the

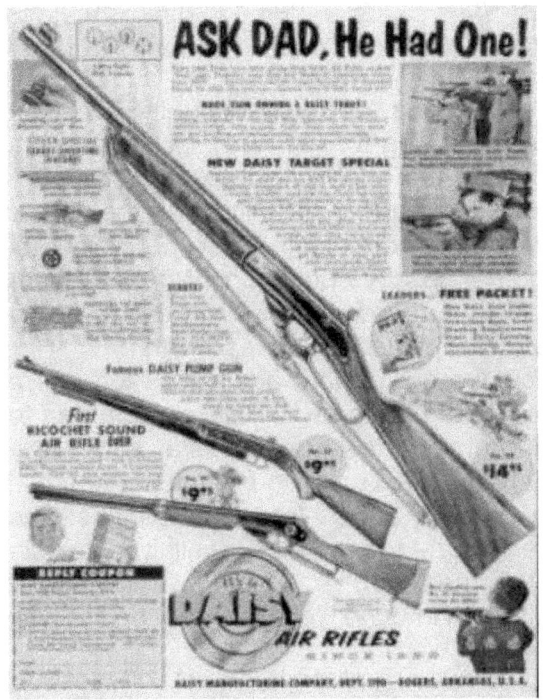

main path, but one aisle or pathway over. Evidently, he was contemplating the same thing I was, "How do you cross this 'No man's land' and do it safely."

As I stood up, I immediately got the attention of one of the maintenance crew; and, because of that, I got Dicky's attention as well.

"Hey, you." The maintenance guy yells. At about the same time the maintenance guy sees Dicky rise up, get on one knee and fires his air rifle. BANG! The loud noise was accompanied by this thick cloud of smoke. Both added to the realism of a real rifle being fired.

I do a head-over-heals tumble, making sure I tuck my head (learned the technique from my brother Wayne who is a stuntman) and then land flat on my back. To add to what I thought would be realistic, I let go of my rifle as it went careening in the air. Realism, realism, is what we go for. And besides, we had some newbies watching.

"What did you do? You shot him. Is he dead?" The maintenance guy yells at Dicky.

Evidently, I had just pulled off an Oscar performance of being shot while running; the maintenance guy was really excited and concerned. The maintenance guy runs over to where I lay. Now I'm in a dilemma. Do I just get up, get my rifle and get outa Dodge or do I lay there, act like I'm hurt? Nope, can't be caught and be put in the hands of the true enemy. As the maintenance guy gets closer, I jump up get my rifle and yell, "Code Red."

The maintenance guy startled that I even moved was even more stunned when I yelled "Code Red" and multiple bodies started popping up all over the place. Code Red was our signal to cease all activity and head to our designated rallying point. As we all revealed our location and began running, the other maintenance guys began shouting. It was glorious. They had no clue we were in the garden and added their surprise when we all popped up and began running.

"One day we are gonna get you. We're gonna catch all you guys. Just wait." The maintenance guys were yelling at us but laughing the whole time. We made their day.

We made it back to the rendezvous point, all accounted for. Our faces were flushed, and we were gasping for air. We just did about a 100-yard dash. The newbies were thoroughly impressed. We did a debrief of what happened and how we could be stealthier in the future. We didn't originally think what would happen after the first shot was fired; and that it would get the maintenance guys attention (What? We are kids, we don't think of everything you know). However, the resulting activity and interaction with the maintenance crew was worth it.

"OK, we had our fun. Now we got to do it again, this time as a team, and we can't be seen. We got to go through the Rose Garden to get to the Amory, which is on the other side. Stay low, stay silent stay alert. We have done this many times before, it can be done (We could have walked around the Rose Garden, but as I said, we're kids; and besides, what fun is that?). When we get to the Amory, well, it is a whole new world. You'll see." Dicky told the group.

With that, we began our filtration into the Rose Garden, on the way to the Armory.

www.ingramcontent.com/pod-product-compliance
Lightning Source LLC
Chambersburg PA
CBHW050303120526
44590CB00016B/2472